Cook Happy
Cook
Healthy

FEARNE COTTON

Cook Happy Cook Healthy

Delicious recipes to make
life just that bit healthier
and a lot easier

For Arthur, Lola, Rex & Honey

CONTENTS

INTRODUCTION

Welcome to my kitchen. It's full of people, drenched in noise, and a bit of a mess. It's the engine room of our house where everyone congregates at breakfast time, for catch-ups over cake and tea, and to create a bit of clutter whilst cooking as a family.

In the last five years my life has changed a lot. At 29 I was a single girl who worked long days but loved going out to gigs most nights. I'd eat out in the evenings or sometimes skip dinner altogether for a few gin and tonics. It was most definitely a chaotic food routine.

Now I find myself a 30-something wife and mum of two children and two stepchildren. I've reached a point where I want my food to make me feel GREAT, and to have fun whilst making it. For me having a family means eating together and having fun cooking and baking. I still love going to gigs and I adore my job but keeping myself, my family and my friends fed and happy is of paramount importance.

As with a lot of modern families, everyone in mine has different tastes and needs around meal times. For those of us who are parents, there can be a lot of ingredient-juggling and sometimes there's little time to prepare and eat good nutritious meals together. I haven't eaten meat since I was 11 but in my twenties I decided to start eating fish to help get more protein in my diet. I now love to cook fish but have no desire to eat meat again. My husband Jesse eats a mainly pescetarian diet but does enjoy the odd burger now and then. I cook the kids meat because I want them to decide

for themselves when they're older how they choose to eat. My mum is vegetarian but my dad loves a sneaky bacon sarnie, whilst my friends all vary from vegan to carnivore. We all want and need different things, and often there doesn't seem like there's enough time to consider everyone's requirements.

At weekends or quieter times cooking doesn't have to be a crazed rush. I find cooking and particularly baking the most cathartic of hobbies and adore coming up with mad concoctions with my stepdaughter Lola and son Rex.

Cooking and baking come in two different forms: for necessity and for fun. Either way, whatever I'm cooking at home, I like to do it in a healthy way where possible. This doesn't have to be boring or overly expensive, but it will make you, your family and friends feel so much better.

I try to keep away from refined sugar as much as I can and I try to reduce the kids' intake where possible. This isn't always easy but replacing some of their sweet treats with delicious alternatives using natural sweetners is so much better for them in the long run. These days there are so many wonderful ways of making something sweet without touching the devilish white stuff, and eventually you will stop craving the naughties in favour of the healthier alternatives. I want to know EXACTLY what I'm putting in my body and I use as many wholesome, natural and vitalising ingredients as I can. Processed food can DO ONE! Your body doesn't like it on the day you've eaten it and it certainly doesn't like it long term. Most of the food you put into your body should have ingredients that make your skin glow, your hair shine, your body feel energised, your eyes bright and your kids and friends happy.

This book is full of delicious recipes for any time of day, from breakfast on the go to special nights in and rowdy Sunday lunches with your nearest and dearest. Preparing your food from scratch will take a bit more planning than rushing out to buy a floppy sandwich at lunchtime, but by investing the time in making your meals, it will give you a day where you feel full of energy and alert. It'll work out cheaper in the long run too.

When you're busy with work, family and life in general, it can seem impossible to find this time and I suggest lots of ways to 'cook smart', whether that's making dishes in batches that can be frozen or giving tips for leftovers. Getting the whole family involved will make dinner time more fun and you will teach your kids an understanding of good food.

Happiness is definitely a big part of this book. If you're eating things that benefit you physically it will most definitely improve your mood too. In this day and age, when life is so fast-paced, it can be easy to forget how intrinsically linked the body and mind are. We often view them as two separate entities working alongside each other at different rates. Your mind, body and soul are all one big melting pot of wonder that makes YOU who you are, so let's keep them ALL happy. Eating well means your body will be happy, your brain will be happy and YOU will be happy. Isn't feeling full of joy, contentment and happiness what we are all striving for? I believe good, nutritious food has a lot to do

with this. Being on a restrictive and bland diet to lose weight will never make you happy. Eating lots of fried, sugary and processed foods for a quick buzz doesn't offer long-term happiness and worrying about what you're eating the whole time will dull any sign of joy in a second. We are all joy seekers so let's get in the kitchen, cook happy and cook healthy, and feel the love.

MY STORE
CUPBOARD

In addition to fresh ingredients, here are some pantry essentials I use every day and couldn't live without. If you've never heard of quinoa, don't know your gojis from your chias and think maca is a member of The Beatles, don't worry. Cooking and baking with these ingredients doesn't have to be scary, it's just different. Most of these foods are available to buy in your local supermarket, or you might consider buying them in bulk online, which tends to work out cheaper in the long run.

One major change I've made in my own diet over the past few years is to cut out refined sugar, and this has had a knock-on effect on how I cook and in particular how I bake. Getting rid of refined sugar from my diet wasn't necessarily easy but once I was in the swing of things I noticed so many positive changes in my energy levels, focus and mood. I had dabbled in giving up a few times over the years but after the birth of my son, Rex, I wanted to feel light and active again. For me, giving up sugar was the answer. Fear not though, this doesn't mean you can't have divine treats. Once you've got your head around why each ingredient is so gorgeous for your body and mind, you'll never look back.

NUTS, SEEDS AND DRIED FRUITS

NUTS

As I don't eat meat, nuts play an important role in my diet as they are full of protein. They are the handiest little pantry fallback and I often grab a handful to keep me going when I'm on the run. I use them for almost everything from scattering them on salads, as a flour alternative in cakes and even to make a milk substitute. My favourites are almonds, cashews, pecans, walnuts and hazelnuts, and I always buy the unsalted kind.

CHIA SEEDS

I've come to love these nutritious little gems, which contain more omega-3 fatty acids than any other seed. They can be used to make energy-boosting breakfasts, help bind cakes together like an egg or be sprinkled in a smoothie. They're packed with antioxidants that help your body and your brain.

PUMPKIN SEEDS

These sensational seeds are full of magnesium, which is great for blood pressure and all-round maintenance for your body. They have a distinct and delicious flavour, which works well in energy bars, granola and even soups. You can buy them in most supermarkets and they can be stored in a glass jar ready to snack on or to use in recipes.

DRIED APRICOTS

These fibre-rich beauties are bursting with sweet juicy flavour, adding a bit of sunshine to your stews, biscuits and cakes. I always use the preservative-free unsulphured kind which are darker in colour and are a little coarser than their sulphured counterparts.

GOJI BERRIES

Oh how I love the goji. For me it's all about getting the most out of your foods and these guys cram in a tonne of vitamin A and are a helpful friend to your immune system. They taste delicious and I often snack on them as they come, but they're also fantastic in porridge, smoothies and even some savoury dishes.

MEDJOOL DATES

These are the king of dates. Juicy, hearty and so soft, they're perfect for energy balls and bars as they hold everything together so well and create a natural sweetness. Use them in smoothies as a sugar substitute or enjoy one in a decadent mouthful as a snack.

OILS AND PASTES

COCONUT OIL

This is definitely the most frequently used ingredient in our kitchen. If we run out of the stuff it's a family emergency. We cook most of our food in it, I melt it down to use in cakes and sweet recipes, and I even use it on my skin as a cleanser or moisturiser. I find it a much cleaner and lighter way to cook with so many health benefits. Long live the coconut!

OLIVE OIL

The cornerstone of the Mediterranean diet is praised for its nutritious properties and proven to contribute to some of the healthiest communities in the world, its most famous asset being that it's said to lower the risk of heart disease. Healthy fats are essential in your diet, and this is a versatile oil which you can cook with or drizzle on dishes.

TAHINI

This rich sesame paste is a genius addition to energy balls, dressings and marinades and offers up more protein than most nuts. It's packed full of flavour and really beefs up a dish when used in a dressing or dip.

FLOURS, GRAINS AND PULSES

RICE FLOUR

This is a brilliant white flour substitute with the added bonus that it's free from gluten, so can be enjoyed by coeliacs. You can buy both white and brown rice flour, and I find they taste quite similar to wheat flour when used in sweet and savoury dishes.

SPELT FLOUR

Spelt may be slightly more pricey than your average white flour but it's so worth it due to its health benefits. Full of dietary fibre and nutrients, you can use it to make delicious loaves of bread, cakes and biscuits too.

WHOLEGRAIN FLOUR

Wholegrain is a much more nutritious choice than the classic white flour. It hasn't undergone the extreme processing that white flour has, so retains much of its goodness. Wholegrains are kind to the bowel and blood pressure and release their energy in a slower and more efficient way than processed carbohydrates. It's an easy swap to make, and tastes delicious too.

QUINOA

I use quinoa a lot in my recipes and it's a fantastic alternative to starchy carbohydrates like white rice and pasta. When it's in the packet it looks terribly boring and worthy, but it's what you do with it that counts. Quinoa is easy to cook, full of protein and is wheat- and gluten-free. It can be creamy and fluffy or crunchy and nutty depending on how you cook it. This is one of the most versatile of all ingredients, which is why I love it.

LENTILS AND CHICKPEAS

These may look humble, but they are the super heroes of the legume family. They are low fat and packed with complex carbohydrates, protein and fibre, assisting your cardiovascular system and all-round health. They're incredibly hearty so fill you up nicely and can be used in stews, soups and salads to give more bulk and warming flavour. If you are cooking them from dry you will need to soak them in water overnight and drain and rinse before using.

DAIRY ALTERNATIVES

ALMOND, OAT AND RICE MILKS

I've never been a huge fan of cow's milk especially as I do a lot of talking for a living, and dairy and a clear voice don't go hand in hand. Instead I love using almond, oat and rice milks, and use them in the same way as you would cow's milk. Having these available in most supermarkets make them a viable alternative, and in my opinion, they're often more delicious.

COCONUT MILK

This slightly sweet vegan delight comes from the flesh of the coconut. Generally found in tins, its rich creaminess is glorious in recipes from curries to cakes.

TOFU

This soya bean product gets a bad rap, probably because it's so often cooked badly or not marinated properly. It's a great source of protein, which is an important nutritional staple in many vegetarian diets. I use firm tofu for stir-fries and stews and the silken variety in desserts to create a mousse-like texture.

SWEET THINGS

COCONUT SUGAR

This is a gorgeous natural sweetener that is more nutritious than white sugar, and works beautifully in cakes and biscuits. Its nuttiness is similar in taste to brown sugar but it has caramel notes to it as well.

HONEY

I love this sweet amber liquid so much I named my daughter after it. With so many different varieties and flavours of honeys out there you can experiment with different types.

MAPLE SYRUP

Maple syrup is a fantastic sweetener that works brilliantly in a variety of desserts. It is lower in calories than honey and has a slightly woody taste that gives a warm sweetness.

MY GO-TO EXTRAS

CHLORELLA POWDER

Chlorella is an algae which is very green in colour and comes in powder or tablet form. I adore the taste though I know it's not for everyone. Whether you love it or not, it's definitely worth giving it a try in your morning smoothie as it has so many body boosters in one shot. It helps detoxify, assists hormones and aids the cardiovascular system too. It should be avoided during pregnancy and breastfeeding.

MACA

Maca comes in powder form and is lovely in smoothies, soups and protein balls. It has a rich, warm flavour and is a plentiful source of minerals and vitamins, notably B12 which is so important for vegetarians who don't get it from meat. It is also known as a libido enhancer! It should be avoided during pregnancy and breastfeeding.

RAW CACAO POWDER

This will give you that rich chocolately taste in sweet treats and drinks but without the sugar. It is the raw form of cacao in chocolate that contains all the antioxidants so it's significantly more healthy than the more common cornershop confectionery. On its own it tastes bitter but it can be sweetened with maple syrup or honey. I'm a full-blown chocoholic so I always keep a stash of this at home.

SEA SALT

Sea salt hasn't undergone the extensive processing that table salt has so still holds lots of vital minerals important for your body. You can use it in so many ways to liven up a dish, and even in your sweet dishes.

Breakfast. To some a NEED, a want, a must. To others, the unthinkable. I fit into category A and will always have love in my heart and tummy for an early fuel-up. Without it I quickly descend into a moody, agitated and withered wreck.

If you've never been a breakfast lover, now is the time to start giving it a chance. It doesn't have to be a time-consuming or huge meal, but make it count so you start your day as you'd like it to continue. I spent years rushing out of the door ready to battle my way through traffic with unbrushed hair and one shoelace undone, but I'd always make sure I had some breakfast in me.

In my 1980s childhood, breakfast was always high-sugar cereal and toast with jam, but now the breakfast arena has opened up to new excitement.

These days I often arrive at work with some Tupperware, packed with oats I have soaked the night before, spelt bread with nut butter, or fruit and coconut yoghurt. All super-quick to assemble yet massively appreciated once at work.

As long as that first meal is packed with slow-burning energy and nutrients you're good to go. In the UK we are kings of the fried breakfast, and now even this can be a healthy option with a twist to the techniques and ingredients.

Now I have kids, breakfast time is one of the most fun yet chaotic mealtimes. With an age range that spans from a baby to a 14-year-old, it's all going on: some are off to school, and some are trying food for the first time. We have to be organised and militant about that first hour of the day during the week when my stepchildren are with us, but at weekends, breakfast has always been a different kind of love affair. This is the time to scoot around in your PJs and slippers rustling up eggs or decadent pancakes piled with fruit. If you happen to have a wonderful partner in your life, perhaps they would even do this for you so you can enjoy breakfast while you're still snug under your duvet.

So give breakfast a chance and make it count!

Breakfast

CHIA SEED BREAKFAST PUDDING

WITH BERRIES AND YOGHURT

SERVES 4

When my friend Amanda introduced me to chia seeds I laughed as she explained how delicious and creamy this bowl of frogspawn-like mixture was. The next morning, when I approached the bag of seeds she had left me, it exploded all over the floor and I was sure chia and I were just not meant to be.

But these days, we get on very well. With these tiny seeds it's all about what you do with them. Their health properties are impressive: they are packed with omega-3 fats, protein and fibre, to name just a few benefits. But how do you make them delicious? Soaking them in nut milk or coconut water is a great start and then you can build up a divine little pudding with layers of fruit and crunch, and store it in a jam jar ready to take to work or eat on the go.

80g chia seeds

650ml almond milk (page 50 or shop-bought), rice milk or coconut water

4 tbsp yoghurt (coconut, Greek or soya yoghurt all work well)

2 tsp vanilla extract

2 tbsp maple syrup, plus extra for drizzling

½ tsp ground cinnamon

200g mix of blackberries and raspberries

1 tbsp toasted flaked almonds

Combine the chia seeds, milk (or coconut water), yoghurt, vanilla extract, maple syrup and cinnamon in a bowl. Divide the mixture between 4 jars, cover and chill for at least 6 hours, or ideally overnight, until the seeds have doubled in size.

When ready to serve, remove the lids and top the chia mixture with the berries and flaked almonds, and a little drizzle of maple syrup.

MEXICAN EGGS

SERVES 4

I love Mexico and have had some of my favourite meals of all time there. This is the perfect lazy weekend breakfast. If you wanted to prove yourself to be 'partner of the year', serve this in bed on a tray to your loved one. This is also an impressive dish if the masses have descended on your house after a big night out. Eggs are the ultimate brekkie champ as they're extremely versatile, and eating protein is a brilliant way to start your day. I am a bit of a coward when it comes to spice levels, but you can make this as hot or as mild-mannered as you like.

4 tbsp olive oil

1 red onion, halved and finely sliced

5 cloves garlic, crushed

1 courgette, cut into 1cm cubes

1 tsp sweet smoked paprika

½ tsp ground cumin

½ tsp ground cinnamon

1 red chilli, halved lengthways, deseeded and thinly sliced

½ tsp dried chilli flakes

400g can chopped tomatoes

400g cherry tomatoes, halved

8 eggs

Small bunch of fresh flat-leaf parsley or coriander leaves, roughly chopped

Sea salt and freshly ground black pepper

Sourdough bread, to serve

Heat the olive oil in a large frying pan (with a lid) over a medium heat. Add the onion, garlic, courgette, paprika, cumin, cinnamon, most of the fresh and dried chilli (retaining some to garnish) and a large pinch of salt and pepper. Sauté gently for about 10 minutes until softened, then add the canned and fresh tomatoes. Bring to the boil, then reduce the heat to medium and simmer for 5 minutes, stirring occasionally, until the sauce has reduced a little. Taste and season again, if necessary.

Make 8 small wells in the mixture, crack in the eggs and season them with a little salt and pepper. Cover and cook over a low heat for 4–5 minutes (for slightly runny yolks). (If your frying pan is not large enough, pour half the tomato base into a second frying pan, and cook 4 eggs in each.) Once the eggs are cooked to your liking, remove the lid and scatter over the parsley or coriander and the remaining dried and fresh chilli. Bring the pan to the table and serve at once with the sourdough bread to mop up all the delicious sauce.

SPELT & GOJI BERRY LOAF

MAKES 8–10 SLICES

This has to be the easiest loaf you'll ever make. Don't be scared if you haven't made bread before, as this recipe takes all the hassle out of the process but tastes incredible. I love to eat it in the morning, spread with nut butter (page 30).

Coconut oil, for greasing
480g wholegrain spelt flour
1 tsp baking powder
1 tsp bicarbonate of soda
1 tsp sea salt
80g pumpkin seeds
40g dried apricots, finely chopped, or raisins
40g goji berries
1 tbsp honey
520ml tepid water

Preheat the oven to 200°C/180°C fan/400°F/Gas mark 6. Lightly grease a 1kg loaf tin and line it with baking parchment.

Combine all the dry ingredients, including the seeds and fruit, in a bowl, then add the honey and water and mix again until just combined.

Pour the mixture into the prepared loaf tin and bake in the oven for 50 minutes, then carefully remove the loaf from its tin and continue to bake the loaf upside down directly on the oven rack for a further 10 minutes. (This gives it a better crust.)

Remove the loaf from the oven and leave it to cool completely before cutting (otherwise all the steam escapes, resulting in a drier loaf). Once cool, cut into slices and spread with your favourite topping. This will keep in an airtight container for up to 3 days or in the freezer for up to 2 months.

WRAP-AND-ROLL 5-MINUTE BREAKFAST WRAP

SERVES 2

During the week, who has time to linger in the mornings? No one, that's who. We would surely all rather have just a few more minutes in bed. This is the ultimate breakfast for those of us out there who like to press the 'snooze' button more than once; a quick and easy wrap that can be eaten on your way to work or while dashing round the house getting what you need for the day. You're getting protein, veggies and healthy carbs in one meal, making it an ideal low maintenance breakfast that will keep your energy levels constant until lunchtime.

2 tsp coconut or olive oil

4 eggs, beaten

100g spinach leaves, rinsed and drained

2 spelt or wholegrain tortillas (gluten-free if you prefer)

1 ripe avocado, halved, stone removed, and flesh sliced

100g roasted red peppers from a jar, drained and cut into strips

1 red chilli, halved lengthways, deseeded and thinly sliced (optional)

A few fresh flat-leaf parsley leaves, roughly chopped

Sea salt and freshly ground black pepper

Put the oil in a frying pan over a low–medium heat. Add the eggs and spinach and cook gently, stirring frequently, for 4–5 minutes, until you have silky scrambled eggs and the spinach has wilted. Season with salt and pepper to taste, then pour off any excess liquid from the pan.

Place a dry frying pan over a high heat. Warm the tortillas for about 30 seconds on each side or until softened.

Divide the egg and spinach mixture between the two tortillas, top with the avocado, red pepper strips, chilli (if using) and parsley. Season with a little salt and pepper, then fold over the tortillas to enclose the filling and eat straight away.

QUINOA PORRIDGE
WITH APPLE, BLUEBERRIES AND DRIED CRANBERRIES

SERVES 4

My local café started serving a similar breakfast, and I was desperate to recreate it at home so I could eat it whenever I wanted. It's so delicious and a wonderful variation on porridge. Quinoa is such a versatile ingredient and amazing both sweetened as well as used in a savoury way. It's such a powerful breakfast fuel, full of protein to sustain your energy for the day. You can experiment with toppings using whatever fruit, nuts and seeds you have at home, but I love adding sliced apple, blueberries, goji berries and pecans to mine.

200g quinoa, rinsed

400ml full-fat coconut milk

1 tsp vanilla extract

½ tsp ground cinnamon

Pinch of sea salt

1½ tbsp maple syrup or honey

1 dessert apple, cored and chopped into small pieces (skin on)

80g blueberries

1 tbsp goji berries

Small handful of roasted pecan nuts

Bring 800ml water to the boil in a pan (with a lid). Add the quinoa, bring back to the boil, then cover, reduce the heat to low and simmer until all of the water has been absorbed. Stir in the coconut milk, vanilla extract, cinnamon and salt. Simmer gently, covered, until most of the coconut milk has been absorbed and the quinoa has the consistency of creamy porridge. Remove from the heat, stir through the maple syrup or honey, spoon into bowls and top with the apple, blueberries and dried cranberries.

BREAKFAST MUFFINS

MAKES 12 MUFFINS

Muffins don't have to be laden with sugar giving you a rush first thing in the morning, but leaving you hungry and lethargic by 11am. This savoury muffin will give you a good start to the day and it tastes heavenly. The spelt flour is rich in nutrients and there's the added benefit of vitamin C in those juicy tomatoes. The cheese gives them a delightful creamy flavour and adds a boost of protein, too. This is also a convenient bit of batch baking where you can whip some up on a Sunday evening to enjoy at the start of the working week (reheat them before serving, if you like).

1 tbsp coconut oil

200g cherry tomatoes, finely chopped, plus 18 cherry tomatoes, halved, for topping

3 cloves garlic, crushed

350g white spelt flour

1 tsp baking powder

1 tsp bicarbonate of soda

½ tsp fine sea salt

½ tsp freshly ground black pepper

1 tsp sweet smoked paprika

40g fresh flat-leaf parsley, including the stalks, finely chopped

50ml extra virgin olive oil

3 eggs, lightly beaten

300ml almond milk (page 50 or shop-bought), rice or dairy milk

200g feta, crumbled

Preheat the oven to 200°C/180°C fan/400°F/Gas mark 6 and line a 12-hole muffin tray with paper cases.

Heat the coconut oil in a frying pan set over a medium heat. Add the chopped cherry tomatoes and fry for 5 minutes, then add the garlic and fry for a further minute until aromatic. Remove from the pan and set aside to cool.

Sift the flour, baking powder, bicarbonate of soda, salt, pepper and paprika into a bowl. In a separate bowl, combine the parsley, olive oil, beaten eggs, milk, feta and the cooked tomatoes and garlic. Fold this mixture gently into the dry ingredients until combined. Do not over-mix as this will make the muffins tough and dense.

Spoon the mixture evenly between the paper cases, then place three halves of the remaining tomatoes on top of each muffin, cut side up. Bake in the oven for 25–30 minutes, or until a skewer inserted into the middle of a muffin comes out clean. Remove from the oven and leave to cool completely.

These taste best eaten on the day they're made but they can be stored in an airtight container in the fridge for up to 2 days.

VEGGIE 'FULL ENGLISH'

SERVES 4

Synonymous with our great nation are the Queen, rain and the 'Full English' brekkie. We do it well and it's something that most people can cook. Even my dad, who never cooks, is in charge of the cooked breakfast at Christmas. If you're a vegetarian, however, this can be a non-event as you're often just left with eggs and beans on toast. I believe a vegetarian Full English can be as hearty and comforting as its better-known brother, and it hasn't got to leave you feeling sluggish either (that's not how I want to start the day). My recipe includes homemade baked beans, which take a while to cook and require soaking overnight, so if you don't have time for that, go for a good quality canned option. Here's to a lighter yet totally delicious Full English.

2 beef tomatoes

Extra virgin olive oil, for drizzling and frying

2 ripe avocados, halved, stone removed

200g baked beans (good quality shop-bought or homemade – see recipe on page 29)

4 eggs

4 slices of rye bread

1 clove garlic, peeled

Small handful of fresh flat-leaf parsley leaves, roughly chopped

Sea salt and freshly ground black pepper

Preheat the oven to 220°C/200°C fan/450°F/ Gas mark 8.

Cut the tomatoes in half and place them cut side up on a baking tray. Drizzle over a little olive oil and season well with salt and pepper. Roast for 20–25, minutes until they are golden and slightly shrivelled.

Meanwhile, scoop out the flesh of the avocados and cut it into thick slices. Place on a plate, drizzle over a little olive oil and season. About 5 minutes before the tomatoes are ready, place the beans in a saucepan over a low heat and warm through.

Heat 2 teaspoons of olive oil in a frying pan and fry the eggs to your liking. Remove from the heat and season well. Toast the rye bread, then scrape the garlic clove over each slice, almost grating it into the toast, infusing it with the garlic flavour. Drizzle a little olive oil over the toast and sprinkle with a tiny pinch of salt and pepper.

Plate up the toast with the beans on top, the egg, tomato and avocado alongside and the parsley scattered over, and serve immediately.

HOMEMADE BAKED BEANS

SERVES 6–8

These beans take a bit of time to make but they're so worth it. As I don't eat meat, I make a veggie version by omitting the bacon and adding half a teaspoon of sweet smoked paprika instead, when you would have added the bacon. These tenacious beans can be stored in jars in the fridge for a week or in the freezer for up to a month so you can make a big batch in one go. Remember to start this recipe the day before, as the beans need soaking overnight. Serve these alongside my Full English (page 26) for a tasty start to your day.

400g dried haricot beans, soaked overnight in cold water

60ml olive oil

2 onions, finely chopped

200g smoked streaky bacon, finely chopped

2 cloves garlic, crushed

400g can chopped tomatoes

50ml maple syrup

60ml red wine vinegar

450ml water

Sea salt and freshly ground black pepper

Drain the rehydrated beans and place them in a large saucepan. Cover with water and bring to the boil over a high heat. Once the water reaches boiling point, reduce the heat to low and simmer gently, uncovered, for about 1 hour, or until the beans are just tender. Drain the beans and set aside.

Rinse out and dry the saucepan, then add the oil and place it over a medium heat. Add the onion and bacon and sauté for about 10 minutes, until the onions are soft but not coloured. Add the garlic and fry for 1 minute, then tip in the tomatoes, followed by the maple syrup, vinegar and water. Stir, bring to the boil, then reduce the heat to low. Add the drained beans and simmer gently, uncovered, for about 1 hour, or until the sauce has reduced and thickened, and the beans are soft. Season the beans generously with salt and pepper to taste. Serve immediately, or leave to cool completely, cover, and chill or freeze.

NUT & SEED BUTTERS

Nut and seed butter is a protein-packed snack that always tastes better homemade. It's perfect for spreading on toast, and a wonderful addition to smoothies and breakfast bowls. The plain nut butter is lovely as it is, but you can play around, adding some extras. A pinch of salt helps to deepen the flavour, or you can sweeten it with a little maple syrup or honey. Cinnamon works nicely too, and cocoa powder is heavenly with hazelnuts and honey.

NUT BUTTER

MAKES 240G

250g raw unsalted almonds, cashews or hazelnuts

Optional extras:
Pinch of sea salt
1 tbsp maple syrup
1 tbsp honey
½ tsp ground cinnamon
1 tsp unsweetened cocoa powder

Preheat the oven to 180°C/160°C fan/350°F/Gas mark 4.

Spread out your chosen nuts on a baking tray and roast them in the oven for 6–7 minutes, or until they are a shade darker and aromatic. You can check them by cutting a nut in half: the centre should be golden in colour. Keep a close eye on them, as they may need a minute or two more or less, depending on your oven. Once roasted, remove the nuts from the oven and leave them to cool completely.

Add the cooled nuts to the bowl of a food processor and blitz for 3–6 minutes (depending on the strength of your processor) until the nuts transform into a creamy, smooth butter. As the natural oils in the nuts are gradually released, they will aid the process.

SEED BUTTER

MAKES 270G

250g raw unsalted pumpkin and sunflower seeds
2–3 tbsp sunflower oil

Preheat the oven to 160°C/140°C fan/325°F/Gas mark 3.

Spread out the seeds on a baking tray and roast in the oven for 4–5 minutes, keeping a close eye on them so they do not burn. Remove from the oven and leave to cool, then follow the recipe for the nut butter above, adding the oil to the mixture in the bowl of the food processor once the seeds have ground down to a rough powder. The oil helps bring the seeds together into a butter, as they are drier than the nuts. The addition of a little salt and a teaspoon of honey works well.

AMERICAN PANCAKES

WITH COCONUT, BERRIES AND MAPLE SYRUP

MAKES 8 PANCAKES
(SERVES 2-3)

Passionately requested/demanded by the kids, it's often pancake day in our house. These healthy yet decadent American pancakes, a revamp of the classic, take hardly any time to make, so they needn't be just for lazy weekends or special occasions. Your body benefits as well as your taste buds, making it the dream breakfast! Everyone in my family has their preferred toppings, but this is my favourite.

140g white spelt flour, sifted

1 tsp baking powder

Good pinch of sea salt

2 eggs, beaten

50ml almond milk (page 50 or shop-bought) or rice milk

50ml coconut water (or another 50ml milk)

Coconut or sunflower oil, for frying

100g berries of your choice, to serve

Maple syrup, to serve

1 tbsp desiccated coconut, to serve

Combine the flour, baking powder and salt in a bowl. In a separate bowl mix together the eggs, milk and coconut water. Gradually mix the liquid mixture into the flour mixture until smooth.

Heat 3 teaspoons of oil in a non-stick frying pan over a medium heat. Once hot, pour in about 3 tablespoons of batter per pancake, so they measure roughly 8cm across. Fry the pancakes in batches, adding more oil to the pan if needed, for 2–3 minutes, until bubbles appear on the surface, then flip them over and fry for a further 1–2 minutes until both sides are golden. Keep warm.

Serve the pancakes with the berries, drizzle over some maple syrup and sprinkle with a little desiccated coconut. Serve immediately.

SUPER-QUICK GRANOLA

MAKES ENOUGH TO FILL
1 LARGE KILNER JAR
(APPROXIMATELY 800G)

I could eat this sweet, comforting granola all day. I try to always have a jar of it in the house, close to hand for a quick brekkie or so I can grab a handful as a snack throughout the day. It's easy and quick to make, and a lovely nutritious way to start your day. By making your own rather than buying the shop-bought stuff you will save money and know exactly what's gone into it. There's no refined sugar, just lots of vitamin C from the goji berries, and plenty of flavour from the spices.

400g jumbo rolled oats
120g pumpkin seeds
40g chia seeds
80g desiccated coconut
120ml maple syrup
1 tbsp vanilla extract
2 tsp ground cinnamon
½ tsp grated nutmeg
4 tbsp coconut oil, melted
80g pecan nuts
4 tbsp goji berries

Preheat the oven to 180°C/160°C fan/350°F/Gas mark 4 and line 2 baking trays with baking parchment.

Combine all the ingredients (except the pecan nuts and goji berries) in a large bowl until the oats are coated in the oil. Spread the mixture out on the lined baking trays and bake for 10 minutes, then remove from the oven, add the pecan nuts, stir the granola, and return to the oven for a further 5–10 minutes, until the oats are lightly golden.

Remove the granola from the oven, stir in the goji berries and leave to cool completely to crisp up. Serve with your choice of yoghurt, milk and fruit. Stored in an airtight container, it will keep well for at least 2 weeks.

One of the main problems for all of us busy folk is getting enough fruit and veg in our diet. We need those vital vitamins and nutrients to make our brains work well, to make our skin glow, to give us energy to live the life we want to live. Those magical natural beauties full of sunshine and positive energy are only ever a good thing.

If you do find it hard to consume enough F&V in your hectic lives, drinking them is an easy, quick and delicious way of doing so. You can cram smoothies and juices with anything you desire to give you that extra kick. They can be a perfect way to start the day or can give you a much-needed boost if you're having an afternoon slump. Here you'll find some healthy and delicious ways of getting those kicks, and some dreamy concoctions you'll hopefully drool over.

I am most definitely not a night owl. Since having kids I find that if I'm not in bed by 10:30pm I'm seriously struggling the next day. I still love the odd night out at a gig or going out for a meal with mates, but these are fewer and further between than the night adventures of my twenties. During those times

I could pull an all-nighter, cover the hangover with a veil of coffee and buzz my way through the day on a caffeine high. I still adore coffee but it's more of a pleasure than a need. I now get my energy from juices and smoothies by day and then I relax into a warm drink before bed on a cold winter's evening.

I've also changed my attitude towards milk. I was never a huge fan of the dairy variety anyway and usually steered clear, but these days, with so many creamy and divine dairy-free alternatives around, I'm back on board.

If you don't eat meat, getting enough protein in your diet will be high on the agenda and nuts can lend a hand in this department. Nut milks are heavenly and so easy to make. They can be quite expensive to buy in supermarkets, so making your own, which really doesn't take that long, will save you money (page 50).

Staying hydrated is so important so why not do it in style and enjoy making these vibrant, life-enhancing drinks!

Drinks

CUCUMBER, KALE, APPLE & LIME JUICE

MAKES 1 LARGE GLASS

The mere smell of this drink makes me feel lighter and fresher. The flavours are clean yet tart, so a wonderful explosion to awaken the soul. Cucumber is the perfect rehydrator, the kale is full of vitamins and iron, and the apple and lime provide the tang to this superhero juice. The perfect juice to start your morning or as a refresher on a hot summer's day.

1 cucumber
150g kale, rinsed and dried,
and tough stems removed
2 dessert apples
(no need to peel or core)
Juice of ½ lime

Put the cucumber, kale and apples through a juicer and collect the beautiful green juice directly into a glass, then stir in the lime juice and enjoy.

PEAR, SPINACH, LEMON & APPLE JUICE

MAKES 1 LARGE GLASS

I feel like the average pear gets a tough deal. For me it's synonymous with a slightly soggy packed lunch. They don't seem very glamorous or celebrated. I often forget to use them in recipes but when I do, I remember how juicy, tender and full-flavoured they are, as well as being a great source of fibre. The milled linseed thicken the juice slightly, and is good for gut health, so they keep things, ahem... moving!

200g spinach leaves
1 ripe pear
1 dessert apple
Juice of ½ lemon
2 tsp milled linseed (optional)

Put the spinach leaves through a juicer, immediately followed by the pear and apple. The weight of the fruit pressing down on the spinach helps to extract the juice from the leaves. Collect the juice directly into a glass, then stir in the lemon juice and milled linseed, if using. Serve immediately.

MY FAVOURITE REFRESHER

I discovered this lovely combination out of sheer necessity. I have suffered with terrible morning sickness with my pregnancies and have gone off a lot of foods. Finding flavours that suit that condition can be tough, but this concoction is truly magical. It can help soothe a harsh hangover, a queasy tum or just be served as a refreshing beverage on a hot day. It's a healthy alternative to soft drinks, and a great BBQ drink, particularly if you add a couple of frozen grapes to each glass, which look great and act as ice cubes.

300ml fizzy water

Juice of ½ lime

2 slices of lemon

2 slices of cucumber

2 fresh mint leaves

Ice cubes, to fill the glass

Simply combine all the ingredients in a glass and enjoy. Or, for bigger groups, increase the quantities and keep in a jug in the fridge (it will keep well for up to 2 days).

WATERMELON & LIME SLUSHIE

SERVES 2

I adore watermelon. As soon as it touches my lips it makes me want to go on holiday and slump in a hammock for an obscene amount of time. This slushie is easy to make and will transport you to a beach in seconds. It looks gorgeous too, with a vivid natural pink colour. You'll drink it all summer long.

400g fresh watermelon flesh, black seeds removed and flesh roughly chopped

4–6 ice cubes

Grated zest and juice of 1 lime

1 tbsp chia seeds (optional)

Small pinch of pink Himalayan salt or sea salt

Place all the ingredients in the bowl of a food processor or in a high-speed blender and blitz for about 1 minute until smooth.

Pour into 2 chilled glasses and serve immediately, with straws.

FIGHTING FIT JUICE SHOTS

COLD-BUSTING CITRUS SHOT

MAKES 4 SHOTS

I always think the best way to combat a cold is by going down the natural route. This powerful little shot has all the elements needed to get you fighting fit. Get juicy and go the natural way.

¼ unwaxed lemon, skin included
1 carrot
5cm piece of root ginger
Juice of 1 orange
Pinch of cayenne pepper

Put the lemon, carrot and ginger through a juicer and collect the juice. Combine with the orange juice and divide between 4 shot glasses, with a pinch of cayenne pepper on top. Serve immediately.

HANGOVER BLAST

MAKES 4 SHOTS

This is a delightful natural tonic to help ease the head, cleanse the system and make you feel fresh as a daisy. You need to rehydrate when you've been drinking, and the cucumber is full of water and refreshing flavour. Ease the pain in one shot!

1 cucumber
5 sprigs fresh mint
Juice of ½ lime
Pinch of ground turmeric

Put the cucumber and mint sprigs through a juicer together and collect the juice. Combine this with the lime juice and divide between 4 shot glasses, with a pinch of ground turmeric on top. Serve immediately.

HONEY & CHAI WARMER

SERVES 2

Being a bit of a granny at heart, I love a warm drink before bed. It's my sweet tooth demanding one last fix before I snooze for the night. This is a wonderful alternative to hot chocolate and is perfect on a cold evening or while camping. The rich flavour of the almond milk marries perfectly with the cinnamon spice to create a drink that'll make the stresses of the day fade away. There's no refined sugar in it, so you won't get an energy spike after drinking it. Keep the cinnamon sticks, as they can be used again.

2 chai tea bags

500ml almond milk (page 50 or shop-bought) or rice milk

2 tsp honey

2 cinnamon sticks

Pinch of ground or freshly grated nutmeg, to serve

Put all the ingredients, apart from the nutmeg, in a saucepan over a low–medium heat. Gently warm through to infuse for a few minutes. Remove from the heat, strain through a sieve into two large mugs and serve immediately with a little nutmeg sprinkled on top.

THE BEST SMOOTHIE EVER!

MAKES 2 LARGE GLASSES

It just is! I was in Ibiza one summer and ordered a smoothie from a beach bar, and it blew my bikini off. I make this for my husband most mornings and it's a great boost if you're experiencing an energy slump. The maca and chlorella aren't essential, though I do think they add to the richness and flavour.

1 ripe banana, peeled, chopped and frozen

5 ice cubes

2 Medjool dates, pitted

40g walnuts

Large handful of kale, rinsed and dried, and tough stems removed

500ml oat milk, almond milk (page 50 or shop-bought) or rice milk

2 tsp chia seeds

1 tsp ground cinnamon

1 tbsp maca powder (optional)

1 tsp chlorella powder (optional)

Place the frozen chopped banana, ice cubes, dates, walnuts and kale in the bowl of a food processor or in a high-speed blender and blitz for 1–2 minutes until finely ground. Add the remaining ingredients and blitz until completely smooth.

Pour into 2 glasses and enjoy.

TROPICAL MANGO & COCONUT SMOOTHIE

MAKES 2 LARGE GLASSES

Mango has to be one of the most popular fruits in our house. It is packed full of vitamin C and antioxidants that help the skin, immune and digestive systems. Its exotic flavours also make you instantly feel like you're on holiday.

1 green dessert apple, cored

5 ice cubes

1 tbsp goji berries

1 tbsp chia seeds

500ml coconut water

1 ripe mango, peeled and stone removed

Grated zest of 1 lime

Place the apple, ice cubes, goji berries and chia seeds in the bowl of a food processor or in a high-speed blender and blitz for 1–2 minutes until finely ground. Add the remaining ingredients and blitz until completely smooth.

Pour into 2 glasses and enjoy.

MINTY MOO: MINT, AVOCADO & LIME SMOOTHIE

MAKES 2 LARGE GLASSES

Named minty moo for its minty taste and creamy dairy-like texture, the magic of this smoothie is that there is no trace of cow's milk. The key ingredient is avocado, which transforms it into a velvety dream of a drink.

550ml almond milk (page 50 or shop-bought) or rice milk

½ ripe avocado, peeled and stone removed

Small handful of fresh mint leaves

Grated zest and juice of ½ lime

2 tsp maple syrup (optional)

5 ice cubes

Place all the ingredients in the bowl of a food processor or in a high-speed blender and blitz for about 1 minute until smooth and creamy.

Pour into chilled glasses and serve immediately.

POST-WORKOUT PROTEIN BOOSTER SMOOTHIE

MAKES 2 LARGE GLASSES

We all need something delicious to look forward to after a sweaty workout. Having this smoothie will help you get through the pain/boredom barrier. It is a good source of protein, helps those muscles to repair, and tastes heavenly.

2 ripe bananas, peeled, chopped and frozen

200g blueberries

2 tbsp almond butter (page 30 or shop-bought)

350ml almond milk (page 50 or shop-bought)

4 tbsp ground hemp seeds

2 tsp vanilla extract

100g kale, rinsed, dried and tough stems removed

½ tsp ground cinnamon

1 tbsp honey or maple syrup (optional)

Place the frozen chopped bananas in the bowl of a food processor or in a high-speed blender and blitz until finely ground. Add the remaining ingredients and blitz for 1–2 minutes until smooth.

Pour into 2 glasses and serve immediately.

OAT MILK

MAKES ABOUT 1 LITRE

My son Rex and dairy don't mix well, so we give him oat milk instead with his cereal in the morning. It's so creamy and full of flavour that when we first made the switch he didn't even notice. I love to use this in smoothies and hot chocolate too.

150g rolled oats, soaked for
1 hour in 1 litre of cold water
4 Medjool dates, pitted
1 tsp vanilla extract
¼ tsp ground cinnamon
Good pinch of sea salt

Drain the soaked oats and rinse them in a sieve under cold running water. Transfer the oats to the bowl of a food processor or a high-speed blender and add the dates, vanilla, cinnamon and salt. Blitz for 1–2 minutes, until the mixture has formed a paste then – with the motor still running – pour in 1.1 litres of cold water until fully combined.

Pour the milk into a cheesecloth-lined sieve sitting over a clean bowl. Use a spatula to encourage the liquid through the cloth then, once most of the liquid has strained into the bowl, squeeze the oat pulp inside the cheesecloth to extract as much of the liquid as possible. Discard the pulp.

Store the milk in an airtight container in the fridge for 2–3 days. Shake the milk before serving.

ALMOND MILK

MAKES 1 LITRE

Nut milk can be quite expensive, but if you make it yourself it's not only cheaper, it tastes nicer too. Creamy and fresh, it's great to drink on its own, amazing in tea and coffee and perfect for baking recipes. Once you've made it a couple of times, you can try the method with other raw nuts, substituting the almonds for hazelnuts or cashews. I use a nut milk bag, muslin or cheesecloth for this recipe, which you can buy inexpensively online or in health food shops, but you can try using the end of a clean pair of tights (I'm not sure an old, worn pair would add to the flavour!).

150g raw almonds, soaked
overnight in 1 litre of water
3 Medjool dates, pitted
¼ tsp ground cinnamon
¼ tsp fine sea salt

Drain the soaked almonds and rinse them in a sieve under cold running water. Transfer the almonds to the bowl of a food processor or a high-speed blender and add the dates, cinnamon and salt. Blitz for 1–2 minutes, until everything has ground down to a paste, then – with the motor still running – pour in 1.2 litres of cold water until fully combined.

Pour the milk into a muslin- or cheesecloth-lined sieve sitting over a clean bowl. Use a spatula to encourage the liquid through the cloth then, once most of the liquid has strained into the bowl, squeeze the almond pulp inside the cheesecloth to extract as much of the liquid as possible. Discard the pulp.

Store the milk in an airtight container in the fridge for 2–3 days. Shake the milk before serving.

HOT CHOCOLATE

SERVES 2

Have you met anyone who doesn't like hot chocolate? I haven't. It has to be one of life's great simple luxuries. I always remember exactly where I've encounter a good one, too: in Rome on a cold New Year's Day, down Portobello Market in West London at Christmas time and THIS recipe on my sofa watching a film with Jesse. This lovely hot chocolate is free from dairy yet it tastes so luxurious. Adding maca powder gives it a gorgeous malty taste and imparts the magical powers that this Peruvian superfood provides. It's great for energy, your skin and hair too. It's not imperative you use it for this hot chocolate, but I think it gives it a much more decadent taste.

500ml almond milk (page 50 or shop-bought) or rice milk

2 tbsp raw cacao powder or unsweetened cocoa powder, plus a little extra for sprinkling

1 tsp maca powder (optional)

1½ tbsp maple syrup

Small pinch of sea salt

Simply whisk all the ingredients together in a saucepan set over a medium heat. Stir the mixture every now and again until it is hot (but don't let it boil). Pour into cups and dust with a little more cacao or cocoa powder.

Lunch. It is so often the more overlooked, rushed and slightly pathetic meal of the day. I feel sorry for lunch.

You'll certainly know what I'm talking about if you work in a busy town or city where you become part of an army of hungry workers elbowing your way through the streets in search of a quick bite that can be eaten while walking/typing/skimming through social media on your phone. Lunch for the busy has become a quick scoff of processed, terrifyingly orange couscous, floppy and meanly-filled sandwiches and wimpy-looking salads all topped up with a bag of crisps, as the main event really wasn't enough.

In my twenties I would rush lunch and go for shop-bought options as I had other things on my mind, like getting back to work or seeking the next adventure, but these days seeing people eat like this makes me feel a bit sad as there are so many tastier and wallet-pleasing ways to eat. This is not food snobbery as I'm not talking about a three-course slap-up meal every day. I'm talking about food thoughtfulness. I want to enjoy what I'm eating and know at the same time that it's nourishing my body and mind.

Okay, so if you are at work or uni each day you will probably have to purchase a rather unglamorous Tupperware box, but you'll get over this when you take the first delicious mouthful of wholesome homemade food. If you start making your own lunch just a couple of days a week you'll feel so much better, save some money and you might notice those around you looking on rather enviously.

I'm a busy mum and often have to leave the house at the crack of dawn, but on the days I'm out and about, making a quick, healthy and delicious lunch is part of my morning routine, much like remembering to brush my teeth. I'm up early with the kids anyway, so while they're happily munching away on their breakfast and creating much mess, I get to business putting something tasty together. The soups in this chapter can be made up at the weekend and frozen in batches and the marinated tofu & avocado salad can be prepped the night before and assembled on the day, making everything swifter. You'll find the other recipes pretty low maintenance too, perfect for speedy and tasty mid-day meals.

Bye-bye processed lunches, hello energy!

Easy Lunches

COURGETTE, BEETROOT, AVOCADO & PESTO SALAD

SERVES 2

I adore pesto with its powerful punch of flavours. A little goes a long way and really makes this dish beyond moreish. Beetroots are such a superhero veg, bursting with vitamins and gorgeous colour. I like to think of the versatile courgette like bacon here, as it's thinly sliced and friend lightly until golden.

1 courgette

2 tbsp extra virgin olive oil, plus extra to serve

1 clove garlic, crushed

2 tbsp pesto, shop-bought or homemade (page 107)

10 cherry tomatoes, halved

2 cooked beetroot, peeled and cut into 2cm-thick wedges

80g mixed leaf salad

1 ripe avocado, stone removed, peeled and flesh sliced

Sea salt and freshly ground black pepper

Using a vegetable peeler, peel the courgette lengthways into thin wide strips, rotating it as you peel. Stop when you reach the core, and slice the core thinly into rounds.

Add 1 tablespoon of the oil to a pan and set over a high heat. Once hot, add the courgette and fry for 2–3 minutes until slightly softened and golden.

In a bowl, combine the oil, garlic, pesto, tomatoes and beetroot. Add the salad leaves and courgette and gently combine. Arrange on a flat serving dish with the avocado slices nestled into the leaves, season with salt and pepper and drizzle over a little more olive oil. Serve immediately.

QUICK QUESADILLA

FOR KIDS . . .
AND ADULTS!

SERVES 4

This is a super way to sneak mushrooms and green vegetables into a child's diet. Most vegetables can be used in this recipe, and chicken also works well, so it's a good one for using up those leftover bits and pieces that lurk in the drawer of your fridge.

3 tbsp olive oil, plus extra for brushing

400g mushrooms, thinly sliced (button, Portobello and shiitake all work well)

100g kale, rinsed, dried, tough stems removed and leaves finely chopped

½ onion, finely chopped

2 cloves garlic, crushed

Small handful of fresh flat-leaf parsley leaves, roughly chopped

4 large corn or flour tortillas

200g Cheddar cheese, grated

100g mozzarella, grated

Sea salt and freshly ground black pepper

Tomato salsa (page 117), to serve (optional)

Heat 3 tablespoons of olive oil in a large frying pan or wok over a medium–high heat. Add the mushrooms and kale, stir-fry for 2 minutes, then add the onion, season with salt and pepper and fry for a further 3 minutes, until the onion is starting to soften. Finally, add the garlic and fry for 30 seconds until fragrant, taking care not to let it burn. Remove from the heat, mix in most of the chopped parsley and leave to one side.

Lay one of the tortillas on a board, add a quarter of the mushroom and kale mixture and a quarter of each of the grated cheeses on one half, then fold the tortilla in half to enclose the filling. Brush the tortilla with a little olive oil, then place in a large dry frying pan over a medium heat. Cook for 2 minutes on each side, until the cheese inside has melted and the tortilla is crisp and golden. Cook the remaining tortillas in the same way, then remove them from the pan, slice them into wedges and serve immediately with the remaining parsley scattered over and the tomato salsa on the side, if using.

LENTIL, HARICOT & VEG SOUP

SERVES 4

This recipe was originally passed down by my friend Heidi's mum, Margaret, and it continues to be a hit. Heidi is someone I go to for 'mum advice', as she is a super-mum to her brood, always cooking lovely meals and getting good food in their mouths. This wholesome soup works well as a quick lunch, taken in a flask to work and eaten over the week, and is freezer-friendly too. Full of veg, but not time-consuming to prepare, it's a winner.

2 tbsp olive oil, plus extra for drizzling

1 leek, trimmed and finely chopped

1 clove garlic, crushed

100g red lentils

1 large sweet potato (about 275g), peeled and cut into small bite-sized chunks

2 carrots, cut into small bite-sized chunks

1.2 litres vegetable stock (page 173) or make it with good quality bouillon powder

100g canned haricot beans, drained and rinsed

Handful of fresh flat-leaf parsley leaves, roughly chopped

Sea salt and freshly ground black pepper

Heat the oil in a large high-sided saucepan (with a lid) over a medium heat. Add the leeks and sauté for 10–12 minutes until softened but not browned. Add the garlic and fry for 1 minute until aromatic, then add the remaining ingredients (setting aside some parsley to garnish). Increase the heat to high, cover and bring to the boil for 1 minute, then reduce the heat and simmer, covered, for 15–20 minutes, until the carrots and sweet potato are cooked through. Season with salt and pepper to taste.

To serve, ladle the soup into bowls, drizzle over a little olive oil and scatter over the remaining parsley.

SALMON FISH FINGERS
& GREEN BEANS

SERVES 4
(MAKES 16 FINGERS)

Fish fingers made a regular appearance when I was growing up, but the homemade version always tastes so much better than shop-bought, and you know exactly what's going in them. You can make these with chicken or firm tofu in the same way, depending on your preference, and enjoy them with the whole family.

300g green beans

1 tbsp extra virgin olive oil

100g cornflour

250g spelt or gluten-free breadcrumbs

500g boneless salmon fillets, skin removed and cut into 16 2 x 7cm fingers

2 eggs, beaten

4 tbsp sunflower oil

1 lemon, cut into wedges

Sea salt and freshly ground black pepper

Mayonnaise, to serve

Bring a saucepan of salted water to the boil, add the green beans and cook for 3–4 minutes, until they are cooked but retain a little bite. Drain, toss with the olive oil and season with salt and pepper. Keep warm.

Combine the cornflour with 1 teaspoon each of salt and black pepper in a bowl. Put the breadcrumbs in a separate bowl. Coat a salmon finger in the flour, then dip it into the beaten egg and finally roll it in the breadcrumbs until evenly covered on all sides. Set aside on a plate while you repeat with the remaining salmon fingers.

Heat the sunflower oil in a frying pan over a medium heat. Add the salmon fingers and fry for 2–3 minutes on each side, in batches if necessary, until crisp, golden and cooked through. Remove from the heat, drain on kitchen paper, sprinkle with sea salt and serve immediately with the green beans, lemon wedges and mayonnaise to dunk the fingers into.

MARINATED TOFU & AVOCADO SALAD

SERVES 2–3

This is a fresh, flavour-packed lunch bursting with health-enhancing nutrients. It's super-speedy to make, and looks pretty too. If you prepare the tofu the night before and leave it in the fridge, this becomes an even quicker lunch to make the next day. You could also double the quantity of marinated tofu, and use the other half to make the tofu casserole (page 171).

400g firm tofu

2 tbsp extra virgin olive oil, plus extra to serve

2 tbsp balsamic vinegar, plus extra to serve

2 cloves garlic, crushed

1 ripe avocado, halved, stone removed

100g rocket leaves

½ red onion, halved and thinly sliced

10 cherry tomatoes, halved

Grated zest of 1 unwaxed lemon

1 tsp poppy seeds

Sea salt and freshly ground black pepper

Gently wrap the tofu in a clean tea towel. Place it on a chopping board and balance another chopping board or heavy plate on top. Leave to one side for 10 minutes to drain.

Meanwhile, combine the olive oil, vinegar, garlic and a pinch of salt and pepper in a bowl. Unwrap the tofu, cut it into 2cm cubes and add it to the bowl. Gently combine with the marinade, cover and leave in the fridge for at least 1 hour, or overnight.

When you are ready to make the salad, simply slice the avocado flesh and combine it with the rocket, sliced onion, tomatoes, lemon zest, poppy seeds and marinated tofu. Season with a little salt and pepper and a drizzle of oil and balsamic vinegar to taste. Serve immediately.

PEA, BROAD BEAN & MINT SOUP

SERVES 4

This is such a lovely dish: it's fresh and light but comforting at the same time, so it works just as well on a cold winter's afternoon as it does for an al-fresco lunch in the sun. It's super-quick to make, so if you have guests arrive out of the blue, or are rushing around, this is perfect. It can be made the day before too and it will keep in the freezer for up to 1 month.

2 tbsp extra virgin olive oil, plus extra for drizzling

1 medium onion, finely chopped

2 cloves garlic, crushed

1 litre vegetable stock (page 173) or make it with good quality bouillon powder

400g fresh or frozen peas

100g fresh or frozen broad beans

5g fresh mint leaves, finely chopped, plus extra to garnish

5g fresh flat-leaf parsley leaves, finely chopped

Sea salt and freshly ground black pepper

2 tbsp full-fat coconut milk, to serve (optional)

Heat the oil in a saucepan over a medium heat. Add the onion and garlic and sauté for 10–15 minutes until the onion is soft and translucent. Add the stock, peas and broad beans, bring to the boil, then reduce the heat a little and simmer for 10 minutes. Add the chopped mint and parsley and simmer for a further 2 minutes, then season with salt and pepper to taste. Remove from the heat and leave to cool for 5 minutes, then transfer to a blender and purée until smooth (or blend in the pan with a stick blender). Return the soup to the pan, and heat through once again. Taste and adjust the seasoning if necessary.

To serve, ladle the soup into bowls and drizzle over a little extra virgin olive oil, and coconut milk (if using). Scatter over the extra mint leaves and serve immediately.

ZINGY MANGETOUT, EDAMAME & SWEETCORN
NOODLE SALAD
SERVES 2

This crunchy zinger of a salad is a filling dish full of flavour and bite. The ginger adds warmth and is packed with properties which are said to aid digestion. I often make a double batch of this so that I can have it for lunch the next day too – it works well thrown into some Tupperware and eaten on the run. You could add in some thinly sliced beef for a meaty version, frying it off before adding the vegetables.

180g rice vermicelli noodles

1 tbsp coconut oil

2 tsp toasted sesame oil

150g podded edamame beans

150g canned sweetcorn kernels, drained

100g mangetout, halved lengthways

4cm piece of ginger, peeled and very finely chopped

4 spring onions, finely sliced

4 tsp soy sauce

2 tsp sesame seeds

Cook the noodles according to the packet instructions, rinse under cold running water, drain and set aside.

Meanwhile, put the coconut oil and half the sesame oil in a frying pan or wok over a medium–high heat. Once hot, add the edamame beans, sweetcorn and mangetout and fry for 3 minutes, stirring. Add the ginger and fry for a further 2 minutes, then add most of the spring onions and fry for a further minute.

Add the cooked noodles to the pan with the soy sauce, most of the sesame seeds and the remaining sesame oil. Toss together until the noodles are hot, then taste and adjust the seasoning with a little more soy sauce or sesame oil if necessary. Serve immediately, scattered with the remaining spring onions and sesame seeds.

SESAME, CUCUMBER & TOFU SALAD

SERVES 2

This is a light and punchy salad that is quick to whip up. Tofu is a great source of protein and works well with the calcium-rich sesame seeds, making this a super-healthy little number. It makes a lovely standalone lunch and also works brilliantly as an accompaniment to meat or fish.

200g firm tofu

1 cucumber

10g chives, snipped into 3cm lengths

60g rocket leaves

A few leaves of salad cress, to garnish

For the sesame dressing:

2½ tsp toasted sesame oil

2 tsp soy sauce

1 tsp maple syrup

1½ tsp cider vinegar

1 clove garlic, crushed

2cm piece of root ginger, peeled and very finely grated

1 tsp toasted sesame seeds, plus extra for sprinkling

Gently wrap the tofu in a clean tea towel. Place it on a chopping board and balance another chopping board or heavy plate on top. Leave to one side for 5 minutes to drain.

Meanwhile, whisk together all the ingredients for the sesame dressing in a bowl.

Using a vegetable peeler, peel the cucumber into long, thin strips, turning it as you go. Stop once you reach the watery core. Place the strips in a bowl.

Unwrap the tofu and cut it into 1cm cubes, then add it to the dressing and toss to combine.

Combine the cucumber strips with the chives and rocket, and divide between 2 plates, with the tofu nestled into the leaves and any remaining dressing drizzled over. Scatter over the salad cress and a few more sesame seeds, and serve immediately.

QUICK & EASY QUINOA BOWL

SERVES 4–6

This is by far the most frequently made recipe in the book, I cook it up at least once a week. Quinoa is a great base for a meal, as it's packed with protein and gives you energy for the rest of the day minus that sluggish feeling. When I've got a busy day rushing around, this is my go-to lunch. You can have fun and switch the veg for any others you have to hand, and add some cheese, chorizo or eggs, too, if you fancy.

300g quinoa, rinsed

3 tbsp coconut or olive oil

½ tsp ground cumin

½ tsp ground coriander

2 carrots, halved lengthways and very thinly sliced

1 leek, trimmed, halved lengthways and thinly sliced

1 courgette, roughly chopped

Large handful of kale, rinsed, dried, tough stems removed and leaves finely chopped

3 cloves garlic, crushed

4 tbsp dried cranberries

2 tbsp roasted cashew nuts

Handful of fresh flat-leaf parsley leaves, roughly chopped

Sea salt and freshly ground black pepper

Optional extras:
Poached eggs
A few slices of chorizo, fried with the vegetables
A few slices of halloumi cheese, fried on both sides until golden

In a saucepan (with a lid), bring the quinoa to the boil in double its quantity of salted water. Once the water has come to the boil, reduce the heat to low, cover and simmer gently for about 12 minutes, until the water has been absorbed. Remove from the heat, stir in 1 tablespoon of the coconut or olive oil, and add the ground cumin and coriander. Leave to one side, uncovered.

While the quinoa is cooking, heat 2 tablespoons of the coconut or olive oil in a large frying pan over a medium–high heat. Add the carrots, chorizo (if using), leek, courgette and kale and sauté for about 6 minutes. Add the garlic and fry for a further minute until fragrant and all the vegetables are cooked through, but retain a little bite. Add the vegetables to the cooked quinoa, together with the dried cranberries, cashew nuts and most of the parsley. Stir to combine and season to taste with salt and pepper. Serve the quinoa scattered with the remaining parsley, or top with poached eggs or halloumi.

RAW SLAW
SALAD

SERVES 2–4

Coleslaw always reminds me of my childhood and brings back memories of buffet-style parties where it would be so rich you couldn't handle more than a teaspoon at a time. This recipe is a much cleaner and fresher version that you can eat by the bucketload if you wish, as it's full of healthy iron-packed greens and natural yoghurt. Enjoy it on its own or as a lovely side to a roast dinner.

40g kale, washed, dried, tough stems removed and leaves finely chopped

200g white cabbage, finely sliced or grated

2 carrots, coarsely grated

Grated zest and juice of ½ lime

3 tbsp coconut, Greek or soya yoghurt

1 tbsp sesame seeds, toasted

1 tbsp extra virgin olive oil

½ tsp dried chilli flakes (optional)

Sea salt and freshly ground black pepper

Combine all the ingredients in a large bowl and season with salt and pepper to taste. Serve immediately.

SCRAMBLED TOFU ON RYE

SERVES 2

Another much-loved recipe of mine, this makes a welcome change from scrambled eggs. Years ago I visited Hawaii and discovered scrambled tofu in a local deli. I haven't found anywhere that serves it in that way since, so I've taken matters into my own hands.

400g firm tofu
1 tbsp olive oil
1 small red onion, halved and thinly sliced
2 cloves garlic, crushed
½ tsp ground coriander
½ tsp ground cumin
½ tsp ground turmeric
200ml full-fat coconut milk
2 slices of rye bread
Extra virgin olive oil, to drizzle
Small handful of fresh flat-leaf parsley leaves, roughly chopped
Sea salt and freshly ground black pepper

Tightly wrap the tofu in a clean tea towel. Squeeze the tofu very firmly over the sink, tightening the tea towel to extract as much water as possible, almost wringing it out. Unwrap the tofu and crumble it into a bowl, breaking up any large pieces with a fork.

Heat the oil in a large saucepan over a medium heat. Add the onion and garlic and sauté for 5 minutes until softened, then add the ground coriander, cumin and turmeric and fry for a further minute until aromatic. Add the crumbled tofu and stir well to combine, then pour in the coconut milk. Simmer for 5 minutes, until the mixture has reduced slightly, and season well with salt and pepper to taste.

Meanwhile, toast the rye bread. Drizzle the toast with a little olive oil and season with a small pinch of sea salt. Divide the scrambled tofu between each slice, scatter over the chopped parsley and serve.

MOZZARELLA, AVOCADO

& CHERRY
TOMATO SALAD

SERVES 2

This is a beautiful but very simple salad, which relies on ingredients that are at their best, so try to use good quality extra virgin olive oil and balsamic vinegar, as it makes a massive difference to the finished dish.

50g lamb's lettuce or rocket leaves

16 cherry tomatoes, halved

1 ripe avocado, stone removed, peeled and flesh cut into 1cm-thick slices

1 ball of buffalo mozzarella, drained and sliced

2 tbsp extra virgin olive oil, plus extra to serve

1 tbsp balsamic vinegar

Sea salt and freshly ground black pepper

Chunks of sourdough or spelt bread, to serve

Remove the ingredients from the fridge at least 30 minutes before you plan on serving, so the tomatoes and cheese can come up to room temperature.

Arrange the lamb's lettuce or rocket, halved tomatoes, avocado slices and sliced mozzarella on a serving dish or 2 individual plates. Season well with salt and pepper and drizzle over the olive oil and balsamic vinegar. Serve immediately with extra olive oil and chunks of sourdough or spelt bread to mop up the delicious juices.

SHAMAN BROWN RICE & VEG BOWL

SERVES 4

This recipe is inspired by a dear friend of mine and Jesse's, Andy, who is the king of heavenly, healthy lunches. It's packed full of veg and protein and can be served as a meal in itself or as a side dish to accompany fish or meat, and the leftovers are perfect cold in a lunchbox the next day.

1 tbsp coconut oil

300g cooked beetroot (not in vinegar), roughly chopped

200g canned kidney beans, drained and rinsed

100g canned sweetcorn kernels, drained and rinsed

2 spring onions, finely chopped

3 cloves garlic, crushed

2 tbsp tamari or soy sauce

400g cooked short-grain brown rice

50g roasted cashew nuts

Heat the coconut oil in a frying pan over a medium heat. Add the beetroot, kidney beans, sweetcorn and most of the spring onions and fry for 3–4 minutes, until warmed through. Add the garlic and cook for a further 30 seconds until aromatic.

Add the tamari or soy sauce and the cooked rice, and mix together until thoroughly combined. Serve in bowls scattered with the remaining spring onions and cashew nuts.

Four o'clock. The weak hour. Lunch seems like an eternity ago and dinner may as well be in a different time zone. A familiar, irritable feeling creeps in and chocolate springs to mind.

I love a snack. It's the much-needed pit-stop where you can regain some energy, possibly some sanity and also just enjoy something delicious without it ruining your next meal. I've always been a big snacker and always had a sweet tooth. When I was a teenager the only thing that would get my legs moving on the 40-minute walk home from school each day was the prospect of hitting up the local newsagent for a bag of sweets, or a chocolate bar, that I would savour on the last leg of my journey.

Back then I could ride the sugar high, dance it off that evening at my local dance school and neither my waist nor mood would alter. I think as you get older these parameters change and you need to make wise snack choices in order to keep the rest of your nutritional intake in check. There's no point creating healthy menus for yourself every day if you go and hit the sugar, with its artificial high, when the day is nearly done.

Snacking used to be referred to in an almost unhealthy context, synonymous as it was with packets of saturated fat-laden crisps, cholesterol-stuffed doughnuts and quickly gobbled chocolate bars. Now snacks can be the clever helper that allow you combat sluggishness and sustain your blood sugar level until your next meal.

All the snacks in this chapter are quick and easy, and many can be made in large batches to last the whole week. Take them in to work or uni and get out that old trusty Tupperware – it'll be so worthwhile come the inevitable snack attack.

Most of these snacks are also excellent for kids, as they don't contain refined sugar and make for a great post-school pick-me-up. The apricot bites are particularly enjoyed by my stepdaughter Lola.

If you're completely new to cooking, these recipes are an uncomplicated introduction to the world of culinary fun, as they are easily achieved and taste amazing. It's time to shun the vending machine for good. Happy snacking.

Healthy Snacks

CRAB, AVOCADO & CUCUMBER BOATS

SERVES 4

One of my husband Jesse's favourites, this snack is quick and easy to assemble and will rehydrate your system whilst giving a hit of protein from the crab and sesame.

1 medium cucumber

100g cooked crab meat (check for any shell fragments before using)

1 ripe avocado, halved, stone removed, peeled and flesh cut into small pieces

1 tsp toasted sesame oil

1½ tsp lemon juice

10g chives, finely snipped

1 tsp toasted sesame seeds

Sea salt, to taste

Cut the cucumber in half lengthways, scoop out the seeds with a teaspoon, then cut each half in half again, this time horizontally, to make 4 cucumber boats.

Combine the crab meat with the avocado, sesame oil, lemon juice and most of the chives and sesame seeds in a bowl. Season to taste with salt, then divide the mixture between the hollowed-out quarters of cucumber and serve on a board with the remaining sesame seeds and chives sprinkled over.

KALE CRISPS

SERVES 6

I eat kale nearly every day as I adore the flavour and the way you can almost feel it doing your insides good. This recipe is a nice way of getting even more of the green goddess into your diet. You can play around with the spices and seasoning to your preferred taste.

1 tsp sweet smoked paprika
1 tsp ground cumin
½ tsp garlic powder
½ tsp onion powder
½ tsp fine sea salt
¼ tsp dried oregano
¼ tsp freshly ground black pepper
200g kale leaves, rinsed and dried, tough stems removed
2 tbsp olive oil

Preheat the oven to 150°C/130°C fan/300°F/Gas mark 2, and line 2 roasting trays with baking parchment.

Combine all the ingredients, except the kale and oil, in a bowl to make the seasoning mix.

Place the oil in a separate bowl. Tear the kale leaves into large pieces and coat them in the oil, massaging it into the leaves with your hands to ensure they are all evenly coated and slightly softened. Sprinkle over the seasoning mix and toss well to coat.

Spread the seasoned kale leaves out on the baking trays, taking care not to overcrowd the trays, or the kale may steam and become soggy. Bake in the oven for 20–25 minutes, until the leaves are dry and almost crisp to the touch, but not burnt. Don't worry if they are not very crisp at this point, as they will become considerably more so once completely cool.

Remove from the oven and leave to cool, then serve up in little bowls, or straight from the tray. Kale crisps are also lovely tossed into a salad at the last moment, so they keep their crunch.

SPICED ROASTED CHICKPEAS

SERVES 4

I always keep a jar of these on the kitchen shelf as they are the ideal snack when you're having an energy-low or need a boost on the run. The flavours really jump out here, giving the humble chickpea new lease of life.

425g tin chickpeas
½ tsp sea salt
2 tbsp olive oil
1 tsp maple syrup or honey
1½ tsp finely chopped fresh rosemary leaves
2 tsp garam masala

Preheat the oven to 210°C/190°C fan/425°F/Gas mark 7.

Drain the chickpeas and rinse them thoroughly. Transfer the chickpeas to a clean tea towel and pat dry (this helps them to crisp up in the oven).

Tip the chickpeas into a bowl and combine with the salt, oil and maple syrup, making sure they are evenly coated. Spread the chickpeas out on a baking tray, and roast in the oven for 18–20 minutes, until crisp and golden. Remove the tray from the oven and mix the rosemary and garam masala with the chickpeas until evenly coated. Leave to cool, then serve.

BLACKBERRY & LEMON
CASHEW NUT SLICES
SERVES 10

These little gems look so pretty with their pastel colours and neat lines (see picture on page 91). They taste as good as they look and contain no nasties, so you can serve these up knowing you're not going to have a sugar high followed by a nosedive an hour later. The nuts are filled with good fats and protein and the fruit gives you a nice boost of vitamin C.

For the base:
100g raw unsalted almonds
100g raw unsalted cashew nuts
90g dried dates, pitted
1 tbsp coconut oil, melted
Pinch of sea salt

For the middle layer:
250g raw unsalted cashew nuts, soaked in plenty of water for 6 hours or overnight
3 tbsp honey
50ml lemon juice
4 tbsp coconut oil, melted
1 tsp vanilla extract
Pinch of sea salt

For the top layer:
150g raw unsalted cashew nuts, soaked in plenty of water for 6 hours or overnight
2 tbsp honey
Grated zest of 1 unwaxed lemon
150g blackberries
3 tbsp coconut oil, melted

Line a 10 x 20cm tin or a 1kg loaf tin with cling film.

First, make the base. Place all the ingredients in the bowl of a food processor and blitz until the mixture forms a paste that sticks together when you press it between your fingers. Tip the mixture into the lined tin, and press it down, compacting the mixture until it is smooth and level. Place the tin in the freezer for 20 minutes to set.

To make the middle layer, drain the nuts and place them in the bowl of a food processor with the remaining ingredients and blitz until completely smooth. Pour the mixture over the chilled base. Smooth the surface and return the tin to the freezer for 20 minutes to set.

To make the top layer, drain the nuts and place them in the bowl of a food processor with the honey and lemon zest. Blitz until the mixture forms a paste, then add the blackberries and coconut oil and blitz until smooth. Pour the mixture over the middle layer in the tin, smooth out and return to the freezer once again for 2 hours to set.

Remove the tin from the freezer, lift out the slab and lay it on a board. Cut into slices and serve immediately. The slices can be stored in an airtight container in the fridge for up to 3 days, or in the freezer for up to 1 month; just remember to take them out at least an hour before serving to defrost.

CHOCOLATE & GOJI BERRY BARS

MAKES 8–10 BARS

Goji berries are a superfood with a super taste that marries perfectly with the cacao in this recipe. Gojis are naturally sweet and full of vitamin C, which will rally your immune system when you feel run-down. These bars are easy to make and handy to store at home for an energy-packed snack. They're a great sweet treat for kids too, with no refined sugar, for a stable release of energy.

160g raw unsalted almonds

3 tbsp coconut oil

20 dried dates, pitted

3 tbsp goji berries

3 tbsp raw cacao powder or unsweetened cocoa powder, plus extra for coating

Line a 20 x 10cm baking tray or 1kg loaf tin with cling film.

Place all the ingredients in the bowl of a food processor and blitz for about 1 minute, until it forms a paste that sticks together when you press it between your fingers.

Tip the mixture into the lined tray, and press it down, compacting the mixture until it is smooth and level. Cover and chill until firm or ready to serve. Once firm cut into 8–10 bars. The bars will keep well in an airtight container in the fridge for up to 1 week, or you can freeze them for up to 1 month.

APRICOT TOFFEE BITES

MAKES 18–20 BALLS

My stepdaughter Lola loves these, so this one goes out to her. The unsulphured apricots give these energy bites a warm toffee-like flavour and gorgeous chewy texture. They're ridiculously quick and easy to make and the perfect antidote to the 4pm slump.

10 unsulphured dried apricots
80g raw unsalted almonds
1½ tbsp coconut oil
1 tbsp almond butter (page 30 or shop-bought)
1 tbsp chia seeds
2 tsp maca or unsweetened cocoa powder

Place all the ingredients in the bowl of a food processor and blitz for 1–2 minutes until they form a paste that sticks together when you press it between your fingers.

Shape the mixture into 18–20 little balls (roughly 1 heaped teaspoon per ball), then place on a tray and chill for 30 minutes to firm up. Store in an airtight container in the fridge for up to 2 weeks or in the freezer for up to 2 months.

NOURISHING BEETROOT DIP

SERVES 4

Naturally brightly coloured food is so good for your body, and it doesn't get much brighter than this. This is a glorious vivid pink dip packed with vitamins from the beetroot and protein from the tahini. Shop-bought cooked beetroot is usually already peeled, but if you're cooking the beetroot yourself, peel them once cooled. This is divine served with vegetable crisps or crudites, on toast or just by the spoonful.

2 tbsp tahini

2 tbsp almond butter (page 30 or shop-bought)

75g walnuts

4 cooked beetroot (about 350g)

2 tbsp extra virgin olive oil, plus extra to drizzle

2 cloves garlic, crushed

½ tsp sea salt

1 tbsp chopped flat-leaf fresh parsley leaves

Carrots, red pepper or any vegetables you like, cut into sticks, to serve

Place all the ingredients, except the parsley, in the bowl of a food processor or a blender and blitz for 1–2 minutes until completely smooth. Place in a shallow bowl, drizzle over a little more olive oil and scatter over the chopped parsley. Serve with sticks of your favourite vegetables, or crisps. Store in an airtight container in the fridge for up to 2 days.

SPICED NUTS

SERVES 4–6

Spiced nuts need no longer be synonymous with a lackluster communal bowl found at a pub. No thanks! These freshly made beauts are wonderfully aromatic, exotic and terribly moreish. I love to serve them at Christmas and often keep them in a little pot in my handbag to snack on through the day.

400g mixed nuts (pecan nuts, brazils, hazelnuts and almonds work well)
1 tbsp olive or coconut oil
3 tbsp coconut palm sugar
1½ tsp sea salt
1 tsp sweet smoked paprika
1 tsp ground cumin
¼ tsp cayenne pepper (optional)

Preheat the oven to 200°C/180°C fan/400°F/ Gas mark 6.

Spread the nuts out on a baking tray and roast them in the oven for about 5 minutes, until they are a shade darker and aromatic, taking care not to let them burn. Remove from the oven and set aside.

Heat the oil in a frying pan over a medium heat. Add the sugar, salt and spices and stir until the sugar begins to melt. Add the nuts and mix them into the sugary spices until completely coated.

Remove from the heat, leave to cool and serve in bowls.

You get in late after a stressful day at work, are exhausted after a full-on day of study, or are in a heap on the floor after picking your kids up from various post-school activities. The LAST thing you want to do is cook a meal from scratch. Quick meals unfortunately often mean unhealthy meals, as you reach for the ready meal, a bowl of sugary cereal or a piece of toast. Let's change that. A wholesome, delicious dinner doesn't have to take up hours of your evening or include trips to different shops for unusual ingredients.

Since starting a family, eating a proper dinner has been the biggest game-changer for me. When I lived on my own I rarely spent time cooking a meal just for myself. I saw it as a waste of energy and time and much preferred meeting up with friends for a quick meal out, or grabbing something on the run. Now I love the traditional family sit-down meal, even if we are all eating variations of the same dish. In most families it's one of the only times you'll all get the chance to chat about the day and enjoy something together.

If you have a family or live with mates, these meals should satisfy the masses. If you are cooking for one, plenty of them can be whipped up after a long day, speeding up that window of time between getting in the door and getting into your PJs! Healthy and speedy don't have to mean boring.

Quick, quick, let's get cooking.

Dinner in a Dash

VEGETABLE PANCAKES
WITH AVOCADO

MAKES 8–10 SMALL
PANCAKES (SERVES 4
CHILDREN OR 2 ADULTS)

These pancakes are a brilliant way of getting vegetables into your kids. They're so tasty and packed with goodness. I give these to my toddler Rex on a regular basis and breathe a sigh of relief that he's had some greens that day. I adore avocados as not only do they taste heavenly, they are so versatile as well, and are great for your skin and hair. The pancakes can be cooked ahead of time, cooled and frozen until required.

Extra virgin olive oil, for drizzling

For the creamy avocado:

1 ripe avocado, halved, stoned and flesh mashed

60g coconut, soya or Greek yoghurt

Grated zest of 1 unwaxed lemon and 2 tbsp of juice

1 clove garlic, crushed

Sea salt and freshly ground black pepper, to taste

For the pancakes:

125g white or wholegrain spelt flour

1 tsp baking powder

100ml almond milk (page 50 or shop-bought), rice milk or dairy milk

1 egg, beaten

75g raw broccoli florets

100g drained, canned corn kernels

¾ tsp sea salt

¼ tsp freshly ground black pepper

1 tsp ground cumin

1 clove garlic, crushed

Coconut or sunflower oil, for frying

Small handful fresh flat-leaf parsley leaves, roughly chopped

To make the creamy avocado, mash the avocado flesh in a bowl and add all the remaining ingredients. Season to taste with salt and pepper, then cover and set aside.

To make the pancakes, place all the ingredients in the bowl of a food processor (except the oil and some of the parsley) and blitz until smooth.

Heat 2 teaspoons of oil in a non-stick frying pan over a medium heat. Once hot, add 2 level tablespoons of the pancake mixture (to make 1 pancake). Fry for 2–3 minutes on each side until golden, then set aside and keep warm. Continue cooking the pancakes until the mixture is used up – you should get 8–10 pancakes.

Serve the pancakes with the creamy avocado on top, scattered with the remaining parsley and a drizzle of olive oil.

ASIAN VEG STIR-FRY
WITH NOODLES

SERVES 2

A stir-fry is such a good option when you're in a rush but want something nutritious and filling. The flavours and crunch in this dish pack a punch and leave you feeling light and invigorated.

150g buckwheat soba noodles (or other noodles)

2 tbsp sunflower oil, plus extra for the noodles

160g skinless chicken breasts (optional), cut into bite-sized chunks

80g tenderstem broccoli

8 baby corn, halved lengthways

1 red pepper, deseeded and thinly sliced

2 cloves garlic, crushed

2cm piece of root ginger, peeled and finely grated

2 tbsp soy sauce

1 tsp toasted sesame oil

1 spring onion, finely chopped

½ red chilli, halved lengthways, deseeded and thinly sliced (optional)

Toasted sesame seeds, for sprinkling

Salt and freshly ground black pepper, to taste

Cook the noodles according to the packet instructions, drain, rinse under cold running water, drain and toss with a little sunflower oil to prevent them sticking. Leave to one side.

While the noodles are cooking, heat the sunflower oil in a large frying pan over a high heat. Add the chicken, if using, season with salt and pepper and stir-fry for 3–4 minutes, until cooked through. Remove from the pan and set aside.

Add the broccoli, baby corn, red pepper and 3 tablespoons of water to the frying pan, reduce the heat to medium–high and fry for 5 minutes, tossing regularly, until the water has evaporated and the vegetables are beginning to soften, but are still crunchy.

Add the garlic and ginger and fry for a further 30 seconds. Finally, return the chicken (if using) to the pan together with the cooked noodles, soy sauce and sesame oil. Toss together and fry for 1–2 minutes until the noodles are hot and have soaked up the liquid.

Serve in bowls with the spring onion, chilli (if using) and sesame seeds sprinkled on top.

HADDOCK BURRITO

SERVES 2

My last meal on earth would go a little something like this. I love the whole ritual of wrapping up the creamy avocado, zesty salad and beautifully cooked fish, and messily devouring one with big mouthful.

1 tbsp olive oil

200g skinless and boneless haddock fillet, cut into bite-sized pieces

1 clove garlic, crushed

½ tsp sweet smoked paprika

2 wholegrain tortillas (gluten-free if you prefer)

100g cooked white or brown rice

½ head of baby gem lettuce, roughly chopped

Small handful of fresh flat-leaf parsley or coriander leaves, roughly chopped

1 lime, cut into wedges

Sea salt and freshly ground black pepper

For the salsa:

200g cherry tomatoes, finely chopped

2 spring onions, finely chopped

½ red chilli, halved lengthways, deseeded and finely chopped

2 tsp extra virgin olive oil

Grated zest and juice of ½ lime

For the guacamole:

1 large ripe avocado, halved and stone removed

1 clove garlic, crushed

1 spring onion, finely chopped

½ red chilli, halved lengthways, deseeded and finely chopped

2 tsp extra virgin olive oil

Grated zest and juice of ½ lime

To make the salsa, combine all the ingredients in a bowl and season to taste. Set aside.

To make the guacamole, scoop the avocado flesh into a bowl and mash it together with the remaining ingredients. Season to taste with salt and pepper and set aside.

Heat the olive oil in a frying pan over a medium–high heat, add the haddock, garlic and smoked paprika, and season with salt and pepper. Fry for 2–3 minutes, until the fish is cooked through, then transfer to a warm plate.

When ready to serve, place a dry frying pan over a high heat. Warm the tortillas, one at a time, for about 30 seconds on each side or until softened.

To assemble the burrito, transfer the tortillas to 2 plates, divide the rice, lettuce and haddock between them and add as much salsa and guacamole as you like. Scatter with parsley or coriander and fold over the tortillas to enclose the filling. Serve the lime wedges on the side to squeeze over.

COURGETTE & CARROT 'SPAGHETTI'

WITH ROASTED RED PEPPERS & MINTY BASIL PESTO

SERVES 2

Is there a more fun kitchen toy than the spiraliser? I think not! The novelty for me has yet to wear off, though you can also make this dish using a vegetable peeler. This recipe works well with pasta as well as spiralised veg, but using courgette in place of spaghetti just increases that much-needed vegetable intake in all our diets. Once you've got the right sauce or dressing you'll never look back, as these vegetables get the perfect makeover.

2 courgettes

1 carrot

2 tbsp olive oil

100g roasted red peppers from a jar, cut into strips

Parmesan cheese shavings, to serve (optional)

Freshly ground black pepper, to taste

For the minty basil pesto:

30g raw unsalted cashew nuts

10g fresh mint leaves

40g fresh basil, leaves and stalks, plus a few extra leaves to garnish

1 clove garlic

75ml extra virgin olive oil

Sea salt, to taste

Preheat the oven to 200°C/180°C fan/400°F/Gas mark 6.

Spread the cashew nuts for the pesto out on a baking tray and roast for about 5 minutes until golden and aromatic. Watch them carefully so they do not burn. Remove from the oven and leave to cool.

Meanwhile, use a spiraliser or julienne peeler to make the courgette and carrot 'noodles'. Alternatively, use a peeler to cut the vegetables lengthways into very thin slices. They can be used like this, or cut again lengthways into thin 'noodles'. Set aside.

To make the pesto, place the cooled cashews in the bowl of a food processor with the mint, basil (retaining a few leaves for a garnish) and garlic and blitz until it has almost turned into a paste. Gradually drizzle in the extra virgin olive oil, while the blade is still turning, until you have a thick and creamy pesto. Season with salt to taste and set aside.

Heat the oil in a frying pan over a low heat. Add the vegetable 'noodles' and most of the red pepper slices and sauté gently for 4–5 minutes, until the noodles have softened slightly. Add 3–4 tablespoons of the pesto, mix together gently, and season with salt and pepper to taste.

Plate up the noodles and remaining red pepper slices, and scatter over the remaining basil leaves and a few shavings of Parmesan cheese, if you like.

BAKED SALMON PARCELS

WITH GRILLED LETTUCE & PEAS

SERVES 2

This meal is nutrient-rich, and makes a lovely light dinner. The sweet marinade for this dish works so well with the vegetables, and the colours all look beautiful together. Lettuce can be terribly boring but by grilling it, you add a whole new level to its flavour and texture.

2 tsp coconut oil, melted

2cm piece of root ginger, peeled and finely grated

2 cloves garlic, crushed

1½ tbsp tamari or soy sauce

2 tsp honey

2 boneless salmon fillets, skin on

200g frozen garden peas

Extra virgin olive oil, for drizzling

1 baby gem lettuce, halved

Sea salt and freshly ground black pepper

Preheat the oven to 200°C/180°C fan/400°F/ Gas mark 6 and line a baking tray with a large piece of baking parchment.

Place a saucepan of salted water on to boil.

To make the sauce, combine the melted coconut oil, ginger, garlic, tamari or soy sauce, and honey in a bowl. Place the salmon fillets skin side down on the middle of the lined baking tray. Pour the sauce over the salmon and use your hands to coat the salmon evenly. Fold over the excess baking parchment and fold it or scrunch it together to create a parcel. Bake the salmon for 8–10 minutes, until just cooked through.

Once the water has come to the boil, add the peas and cook for 3–4 minutes until tender. Drain, toss with 1–2 teaspoons of olive oil and season to taste.

Place a dry frying pan over a high heat. Drizzle 1 teaspoon of olive oil over the baby gem lettuce halves and season them with salt and pepper. When the pan is hot, add the lettuce, cut side down, and fry for 2–3 minutes on each side until softened and charred.

Divide the peas and lettuce between 2 plates, and top with the cooked salmon. Drizzle over any remaining sauce from the salmon parcels and serve immediately.

VEGGIE BURGERS

SERVES 8

Over the years veggie burgers have upped their game. Now there are so many ways of making a tasty patty that's full of flavour and good stuff. These are quick and simple to make and can convince even the meatiest of meat-eaters out there to switch it up for a meal. They can also be assembled, cooked, cooled and frozen, making them a handy freezer fall-back.

125g quinoa, rinsed

2 carrots, coarsely grated

1 cooked beetroot, peeled and coarsely grated

1 large handful of kale, tough stems removed and leaves finely chopped

2 medium eggs, beaten

2 cloves garlic, crushed

20g fresh flat-leaf parsley leaves, finely chopped

1 tsp ground cumin

1 tsp sweet smoked paprika

6 tbsp white or wholegrain spelt flour or rice flour

Olive or coconut oil, for frying

8 spelt burger buns or pitta breads (optional)

Mayonnaise or mustard, to serve

2 heads of cos lettuce, leaves separated, to serve

½ red onion, thinly sliced, to serve

2 beef tomatoes, sliced, to serve

Sea salt and freshly ground black pepper

In a saucepan (with a lid), bring the quinoa to the boil in double its quantity of salted water. Once the water has come to the boil, reduce the heat to low, cover and simmer gently for about 12 minutes, until the water has been absorbed. Remove from the heat, uncover and leave to cool.

Roughly chop the grated carrot and beetroot to make sure the grated strands are not too long, then add them to the cooled quinoa with the kale, eggs, garlic, parsley, cumin, paprika, flour, half a teaspoon of salt and a generous pinch of pepper. Mix thoroughly, then cover and chill for 10 minutes.

Remove the burger mixture from the fridge and shape it into eight 2cm-thick patties. Heat 1 tablespoon of oil a frying pan over a low–medium heat and fry the patties in batches for 6 minutes on each side, until crisp and golden, adding a little more oil if necessary.

Serve the patties in burger buns or pitta bread, if using, with a little mayonnaise or mustard and the lettuce, red onion and tomatoe slices.

DIY TOMATO SAUCE

WITH QUINOA & GREEN BEANS

SERVES 4–6

My best mate Kye texted me recently to ask how you cook quinoa, and what on earth you do with it. It's such a wonderful ingredient, full of protein and massively versatile. This is a go-to meal for me, whether I've had a busy day at work and am ravenous or just need something quick and healthy. Quinoa definitely needs a helping hand in the taste department, so it's very much about how you use it. This delicious sauce adds tons of flavour and veg to the quinoa, to make a light and energising meal.

1 tbsp coconut oil
1 onion, finely chopped
1 courgette, cut into 2cm chunks
2 cloves garlic, crushed
20 cherry tomatoes, halved
400g can chopped tomatoes
60g spinach leaves
300g quinoa, rinsed
100g green beans
60g goat's cheese (optional)
1 tbsp pumpkin seeds
Extra virgin olive oil, for drizzling
Sea salt and freshly ground black pepper

Heat the coconut oil in a saucepan (with a lid) over a medium heat. Add the onion and courgette and sauté for 10 minutes until beginning to soften, then add the garlic and fry for a further minute until aromatic. Add the fresh and canned tomatoes and spinach, cover and bring to the boil, then reduce the heat to low and simmer gently for 15 minutes. Season with salt and pepper to taste, then blend until smooth with a hand blender or leave it chunky if you prefer.

Meanwhile, in another saucepan (with a lid), bring the quinoa to the boil in double its quantity of salted water. Once the water has come to the boil, reduce the heat to low, cover and simmer gently for about 6 minutes, then add the green beans and cook for a further 5–6 minutes, until the water has been absorbed and the beans are just tender. Remove from the heat, and remove the lid to let any remaining water evaporate.

Serve the quinoa and beans in bowls with the tomato sauce spooned on top. Crumble the goat's cheese over the top, if using, sprinkle with the pumpkin seeds and drizzle over a little olive oil. Serve immediately.

SRI LANKAN VEGETABLE CURRY

WITH BROWN RICE

SERVES 4–6

Many moons ago, before Rex and Honey came along, Jesse and I went on a far-flung adventure to Sri Lanka. It is such a vibrant country where the people smile from the heart and the food is made with love. On the entire trip, there wasn't a dish I didn't love. This curry is inspired by the flavours we encountered and the warmth their food provides. I love adding fish to this as it adds an extra boost of protein and makes it even more hearty.

1½ tbsp coconut or sunflower oil

10 fresh curry leaves (optional)

1 onion, finely chopped

5cm piece of root ginger, peeled and finely grated

5 cloves garlic, crushed

½ tsp ground turmeric

½ tsp ground cinnamon

1½ tbsp mild curry powder

½ tsp chilli powder (optional)

1 tsp garam masala

1 tsp sweet smoked paprika

16 cherry tomatoes, halved

2 x 400ml cans full-fat coconut milk

2 carrots, thinly sliced

1 green pepper, deseeded and cut into bite-sized chunks

200g skinless and boneless cod or sea bass fillets, cut into bite-sized pieces (optional)

Sea salt and freshly ground black pepper

1 spring onion, finely sliced, to serve

Cooked brown rice, to serve

Heat the oil in a frying pan over a medium heat. Add the curry leaves (if using) and fry for 2–3 minutes until the leaves begin to crisp up and brown. Add the onion and ginger and sauté gently for 5 minutes, until the onion has softened, then add the garlic and fry for a further minute until aromatic. Add the spices, tomatoes, half a teaspoon of salt and a good grind of black pepper. Fry for a further 2 minutes until aromatic, then add the coconut milk, carrots and green pepper. Bring to the boil, then reduce the heat and simmer gently, stirring occasionally, for 20–25 minutes until the vegetables are cooked through and the sauce has reduced down a little. If you are using fish, add it to the curry for the last 5 minutes of cooking time, until just cooked through.

Serve with the spring onion scattered over the top and rice alongside.

TACOS

You can't beat a good taco, and this is one seriously good taco! I always lay every element of the dish on the table so that people can help themselves, making it a really fun, sociable meal. As I don't eat meat, this veggie version for me is a dream but I've included beef as an option, as Jesse and the kids love it. If you like your tacos very spicy, just add more chilli to suit your taste buds.

2 tbsp olive oil, plus extra
for the beef (if using)

1 red pepper, deseeded and
cut into 1cm-thick slices

1 green pepper, deseeded and
cut into 1cm-thick slices

225g sirloin steak (optional)

4 corn tortillas

1 head of baby gem lettuce,
roughly chopped

1 ripe avocado, halved, stoned, skin
removed and flesh cut into chunks

100g sour cream (optional)

Small handful of flat-leaf parsley or
coriander leaves, roughly chopped

1 lime, cut into wedges

Sea salt and freshly ground black
pepper, to taste

For the spicy black beans:

1 tbsp olive oil

1 small onion, finely chopped

2 cloves garlic, crushed

½ tsp ground coriander

½ tsp ground cumin

½ tsp ground cinnamon

½ tsp sweet smoked paprika

½ red chilli, deseeded (if you like)
and finely chopped

400g can black beans

To make the spicy black beans, heat the oil in a frying pan over a medium heat. Add the onion and garlic and sauté for 5 minutes until soft and translucent, but not coloured. Add the spices and fry for a further 2 minutes, then add the black beans (including the liquid from the can), and simmer for 10 minutes uncovered, stirring occasionally, until reduced, thick and creamy. Remove from the heat and set aside.

To make the salsa, combine all the ingredients in a bowl and season to taste. Set aside.

Clean out the pan you used to cook the black beans and place it over a high heat. Toss the sliced peppers in a bowl with the oil and season with salt and pepper. Once the pan is hot, add the peppers and stir-fry for 5 minutes, until slightly charred and beginning to soften. Remove from the pan and keep warm.

If you are using the steak, drizzle both sides with a little olive oil and season well. Place the same pan you used to fry the pepper over a high heat and, when smoking hot, add the steak. For a steak about 2cm thick, fry it for 2 minutes on each side for medium-rare, or longer if you prefer your steak well done. Remove the steak from the pan and leave to rest for 5 minutes. Once the steak has rested, slice it at an angle into thin strips.

Place a clean, dry frying pan over a high heat. Warm the tortillas, one at a time, for about 30 seconds on each side or until softened.

For the salsa:

2 tsp extra virgin olive oil

200g cherry tomatoes,
finely chopped

2 spring onions, finely chopped

½ red chilli, deseeded and
finely chopped

Juice of ½ lime

To serve, place everything on the table and create your own tacos. Start by putting a few spoonfuls of the black beans on a tortilla, then top with salsa, chopped lettuce, avocado, sour cream (if using), peppers or sliced beef and the parsley or coriander. Squeeze over a little lime juice and enjoy!

Staying in is the new going out, right? Making a meal for your loved one or mates is so much more appreciated than going out to a restaurant, as they know how much time, effort and love has gone into the meal.

Having large groups of friends over can seem daunting as you navigate around their individual likes and food fears, but in this chapter you'll find delicious fuss-free meals to suit everyone's taste. I don't eat meat but I don't expect everyone to adopt my own eating habits when they're in my home, so I happily cook up a few options so that everyone's catered for. Whether you are creating decadent dishes to please the masses or just for a cosy night in for two, you'll find options for vegetarians, fish fans and meat obsessives. They're all meals that are packed with immune-boosting veggies, energy-giving proteins and tons of flavour.

I love cooking but I'm no Nigella when it comes to entertaining. I only wish I could be that relaxed when cooking for a hungry gaggle. My aim here is to create meals that are low in stress for you and high in pleasure for your guests.

I love having lots of dishes on the table so people can help themselves and get stuck into seconds without any embarrassment. Platters and sharing plates also make the table look so pretty, too – a fun frenzy of sharing and scoffing. You'll feel such satisfaction when the recipients of your delicious cooking gasp in delighted astonishment that what they're eating is so good for them, as well as tasty.

Get ready to have a glorious night in!

The Big Night In

MACKEREL

WITH ROASTED TOMATOES, OLIVES & PARSLEY

SERVES 4

To me this recipe always tastes very 'summer holiday'. It features some delicious Italian flavours that make you feel like you could be dining out at a wonderful restaurant whilst abroad. I love mackerel as it's so adaptable and rich in essential oils, and this topping adds a whole other level of flavours into the mix. You could swap the mackerel for another fish – cod and sea bass work equally well.

250g cherry tomatoes

6 tsp extra virgin olive oil, plus extra for frying

1 tbsp red wine vinegar

40g fresh flat-leaf parsley leaves, finely chopped

1 clove garlic, crushed

Grated zest of 1 unwaxed lemon

20 black and green olives, pitted and roughly chopped

4 x 180g mackerel fillets (skin on)

Sea salt and freshly ground black pepper

Preheat the oven to 200°C/180°C fan/400°F/Gas mark 6.

Place the tomatoes in a baking tray, toss with 2 teaspoons of the olive oil and red wine vinegar, season well with salt and pepper and roast in the oven for about 15 minutes, or until the skins split.

Meanwhile, combine the chopped parsley, garlic and lemon zest in a bowl with the remaining olive oil. Add the olives and season with a pinch of salt. While the tomatoes are still hot from the oven, tip them into the parsley oil and stir to combine.

Place 2 frying pans over a medium–high heat. Coat the mackerel fillets with a little olive oil. Season the fish with salt and pepper and place 2 fillets in each hot pan, skin side down. Fry for 3 minutes, without moving the fish, then turn them over and fry for a further 2 minutes until crisp and golden on both sides.

Plate up the mackerel with the tomato, olives and parsley oil on top. Serve immediately.

CHICKEN SATAY SKEWERS

SERVES 4

The kids love these and while I don't eat chicken I could practically drink the satay dipping sauce: it's creamy, nutty and full of goodness. Unlike shop-bought satay sauce, this has no refined sugar and only a small amount of salt, so it's tasty without the sin! Get stuck in!

For the chicken marinade:
4 cloves garlic, chopped
3cm piece of root ginger, peeled
2 sticks of lemongrass, outer layers removed and tender core roughly chopped
1 tbsp vegetable oil
1 tsp toasted sesame oil
2 tsp soy sauce
1 tbsp maple syrup or honey
1 tbsp ground coriander
½ tsp ground cumin
¼ tsp freshly ground black pepper
600g skinless, boneless chicken thighs

For the satay dipping sauce:
½ red onion, chopped
2 cloves garlic, chopped
1 red chilli, halved lengthways, deseeded and chopped
1 tbsp vegetable oil
120ml full-fat coconut milk
3 tbsp maple syrup or honey
3 tsp soy sauce
½ tsp fish sauce (or just use more soy sauce)
Grated zest and juice of 1 lime
120g sugar-free almond butter (page 30 or shop-bought) or peanut butter
1 tsp snipped chives, to serve
Cooked brown or white rice, to serve

Soak the bamboo skewers (you'll need around 14) in cold water for at least 30 minutes, until ready to use.

To make the chicken marinade, place all the ingredients (except the chicken) in the bowl of a food processor and blitz for at least 1 minute, or until it has formed a paste. Transfer to a bowl. Cut the chicken thighs into 3cm-long strips, then add them to the marinade and stir to thoroughly coat the chicken. Cover and chill for at least 30 minutes, and clean out the bowl of the food processor.

To make the satay sauce, place the onion, garlic and chilli in the bowl of the food processor and blitz until it forms a paste. Gradually add the remaining ingredients, and blitz until the sauce is well combined. If it is too thick, add a little more coconut milk, a tablespoon at a time. Taste and adjust the seasoning if necessary.

When ready to cook, thread the marinated strips of chicken on to the soaked wooden skewers, pressing them together tightly. Place a large griddle pan over a medium–high heat and grill the chicken skewers for 12–16 minutes, turning them occasionally, or until cooked through.

Sprinkle the chicken skewers with the chives, and serve immediately with the rice and satay sauce, ready to dip into.

COURGETTE FRITTERS
WITH HUMMUS

Courgette is surely one of the most versatile vegetables out there. I made a huge batch of these when Jesse's band came to stay recently and they went down a storm. If you have any leftovers, just pop the cooked and cooled fritters in the freezer and reheat them through in the oven whenever you fancy.

450g courgettes, coarsely grated

½ onion, very finely chopped

2 cloves garlic, crushed

50g buckwheat or spelt flour

2 eggs, beaten

80g feta, crumbled

Grated zest of 1 unwaxed lemon

Small handful each of fresh mint leaves, flat-leaf parsley leaves and dill fronds, finely chopped

1 tsp ground cumin

4 tbsp sunflower oil

¼ tsp sweet smoked paprika

Sea salt and freshly ground black pepper

For the hummus:

240g can chickpeas, drained and rinsed

80g tahini

juice of ½ lemon

1 clove garlic, crushed

1 tsp ground cumin

3 tbsp extra virgin olive oil, plus extra for drizzling

Place the grated courgette in a colander over the sink and sprinkle over 1 teaspoon of salt. Toss and set to one side for 10 minutes.

Meanwhile, combine the onion, garlic, flour, eggs, feta, lemon zest, most of the herbs and half of the cumin in a bowl.

To make the hummus, place all but 2 tablespoons of the chickpeas in the bowl of a food processor with the tahini, lemon juice, garlic, cumin, extra virgin olive oil and 3 tablespoons of cold water and blitz for 1–3 minutes until smooth and creamy. Season to taste with salt and a little more olive oil and lemon juice, if needed.

Place the grated courgette in a clean tea towel and squeeze out as much liquid as you can. Add the grated courgette to the feta, flour and egg mixture and mix together until thoroughly combined.

Heat the sunflower oil in a frying pan over a medium heat. Add 1 heaped tablespoon of the courgette mixture for each fritter, flattening it out gently to form a rough round shape. Fry for 2–3 minutes on each side, until crisp and golden. Remove and keep warm while you continue frying the remaining fritters.

To serve, spoon the hummus into a bowl, scatter over the remaining chickpeas, the smoked paprika, half of the remaining herbs and a drizzle of olive oil. Plate up the fritters alongside the hummus, with the last of the herbs scattered over. Serve immediately.

PAN-FRIED KING PRAWNS,
FETA, ROCKET & HERB SALAD

SERVES 4

You don't need tons of ingredients to make a full-bodied, satisfying dish and this salad proves that. The zingy, punchy flavours of the dressing go so well with the warm and spicy prawns. Sometimes, the simplest salads are the best.

100g rocket leaves

Handful each of fresh flat-leaf parsley and basil leaves, roughly chopped

50g pecan nuts, roasted (see technique on page 30)

2 spring onions, thinly sliced

10 baby radishes, thinly sliced

120g feta, crumbled

4 tbsp extra virgin olive oil

Juice of ½ lemon

1 tsp wholegrain mustard

2 cloves garlic, crushed

3cm piece of root ginger, peeled and finely grated

2 tsp soy sauce

2 tsp toasted sesame oil

2 tsp honey

2 tsp vegetable oil

300g raw shelled king prawns (tails left on if you like)

Toss the rocket with the herbs, nuts, spring onions and radishes and place on a serving dish, then scatter over the feta.

Whisk the olive oil with the lemon juice and mustard in a small bowl to make a dressing and set aside. In another bowl, mix together the garlic, ginger, soy sauce, sesame oil and honey.

Heat the vegetable oil in a frying pan over a high heat. Once very hot, add the prawns and cook for 1 minute, then turn them over, add the garlic and ginger sauce and fry for a further minute until cooked through.

Scatter the prawns over the salad, then pour over the olive oil and lemon dressing, toss together and serve immediately.

GARLIC BREAD FOCACCIA

SERVES 6–8

This to me is the ultimate comfort food. Garlic is a great immune-booster so as well as tasting amazing, this chunky bread is giving your body a lovely dose of nutrients. I like to serve this warm with olive oil, sun-dried tomatoes and olives on the side. It's also a good freezer fallback and can be frozen for up to 2 months.

500g white spelt flour
2 tsp fine sea salt, plus extra for sprinkling
7g sachet of fast-action yeast
400ml warm water
3 tbsp olive oil, plus extra for greasing and drizzling
1 tsp honey
1 bulb of garlic, separated into cloves (no need to peel)
Handful of fresh rosemary sprigs
Freshly ground black pepper
Sun-dried tomatoes, olives and cured ham (or any other nibbles), to serve

Sift the flour into a large bowl and stir in the salt and yeast, ensuring everything is well combined. Make a well in the centre, add the warm water, olive oil and honey and bring the mixture together with a wooden spoon to form a wet and sticky dough. Cover the bowl with clingfilm and leave in a warm place for 30 minutes.

Once the dough has risen a little, cover one hand with a few drops of olive oil to prevent sticking and knead in the bowl for 2–3 minutes, using a little more oil to prevent sticking, if necessary. Cover and leave in a warm place again for about an hour or until almost doubled in size.

Meanwhile, place the garlic cloves and rosemary sprigs in a bowl, drizzle with enough olive oil to coat and season with salt and pepper. Combine and set aside.

When the dough has almost doubled in size, generously oil a 25 x 30cm baking tray, place the dough in the tray and press it out into all four corners. Scatter over the oiled garlic and rosemary sprigs and use your fingers to push them into the dough, then cover the tray with clingfilm and leave to prove in a warm place for 50 minutes–1 hour, until almost doubled in size again.

Preheat the oven to 220°C/200°C fan/450°F/Gas mark 8. When the dough has risen, use your fingertips to firmly dimple the dough again. Lightly drizzle over a little olive oil and a pinch of salt and pepper. Bake in the oven for 20–25 minutes, or until golden and crispy. To check it's cooked, turn it over and tap the bottom, it should sound hollow.

HALLOUMI & ROASTED BEETROOT SALAD

SERVES 4 AS A MAIN
OR 6-8 AS A SIDE DISH

I could sleep in a bed of halloumi, I love it so much. Its salty taste and chewy texture are a dream combination. Mix it with another favourite of mine, beetroot, and you're laughing: the roasted beets are juicy and tender and work so well with the cheese. This makes a great side salad or sharing bowl for everyone to pounce on.

8 raw, unpeeled beetroot, topped and tailed, cut into 2cm-thick wedges (any leaves retained)

1½ tbsp olive oil

2 tsp balsamic vinegar

300g halloumi, cut into thick slices

½ red onion, halved and thinly sliced

Sea salt and freshly ground black pepper

Small handful of fresh flat-leaf parsley leaves, roughly chopped

For the dressing:

3 tbsp extra virgin olive oil

2 tsp balsamic vinegar

½ tsp honey or maple syrup

½ tsp wholegrain mustard

Preheat the oven to 200°C/180°C fan/400°F/Gas mark 6.

Place the beetroot wedges in a roasting tray, season generously with salt and pepper and toss with the olive oil and balsamic vinegar. Roast in the oven for 40 minutes, until the beetroot is slightly blistered, and tender when pierced with a sharp knife.

Combine all the ingredients for the dressing in a small bowl and set aside.

Heat a large, dry frying pan over a medium heat. Add the halloumi slices and fry them for 2–3 minutes on each side, until softened and golden brown.

Layer the roast beetroot, beetroot leaves (if using), red onion and halloumi on a large flat serving dish, drizzling over the dressing as you go. Scatter over the parsley and serve immediately.

SEA BASS
WITH SWEET
POTATO
MASH

SERVES 4

This creamy sweet potato mash is a wonderful, light but comforting partner for the sea bass. This is a real crowd-pleaser whenever I make it. I cook the fish in a big baking dish, then let guests help themselves.

4 sweet potatoes (about 900g), peeled and cut into chunks

2 tbsp coconut oil

2 tbsp maple syrup

1 ½ tbsp soy sauce

4 boneless sea bass fillets, skin on

2 tsp olive oil

Grated zest of 1 unwaxed lemon and 2 tsp juice

Sea salt and freshly ground black pepper

Small handful of fresh flat-leaf parsley leaves, roughly chopped, to serve

1 tbsp toasted flaked almonds, to serve

Place the sweet potato chunks in a large saucepan, cover with water and bring to the boil over a high heat. Reduce the heat to medium and simmer for about 15 minutes, or until they are tender when pierced with a sharp knife. Drain and mash with the coconut oil, maple syrup and soy sauce, then set aside.

While the potato chunks are simmering, lay a large sheet of foil on a baking tray, big enough to wrap around all four fillets of fish, with room to spare. Place the sea bass fillets on the foil, skin side down, and drizzle over the olive oil and lemon juice. Scatter over the lemon zest and season well with salt and pepper on both sides. Use your hands to coat the sea bass with the seasonings. Fold the foil together to form a sealed parcel and bake in the oven for 8–10 minutes, or until just cooked through.

Spread out the mash on a large, flat serving dish, place the sea bass on top and scatter over the parsley and flaked almonds. Serve immediately.

QUINOA SUMMER SALAD

SERVES 4

Quinoa is a great way of beefing up a leafy salad and adding protein. This dish is a go-to staple of mine during the summer and I make it most weekends when we have family or friends over. It's simple to make, and looks so colourful on the plate.

150g quinoa, rinsed

2 cooked beetroot, sliced into wedges

200g canned or jarred chickpeas, drained

12 cherry tomatoes, halved

½ red onion, halved and finely sliced

50g mixed salad leaves

20g fresh chives, finely chopped

Handful of white grapes, halved

Small handful of fresh flat-leaf parsley leaves, roughly chopped

Small handful of fresh mint leaves, roughly chopped

2½ tbsp extra virgin olive oil

1 tbsp balsamic vinegar

Sea salt and freshly ground black pepper

In a saucepan (with a lid), bring the quinoa to the boil in double its quantity of salted water. Once the water has come to the boil, reduce the heat to low, cover and simmer gently for about 12 minutes, until the water has been absorbed.

Remove the lid and let it cool, then mix in the remaining ingredients, retaining some of the herbs to garnish. Season with salt and pepper to taste, transfer to a serving dish and scatter over the remaining herbs.

TOMATO, PESTO & GOAT'S CHEESE
FILO TARTLETS

MAKES 12 TARTLETS
(SERVES 6)

These tartlets look very impressive but are a doddle to make. I serve them as a starter at dinner parties but they're equally dreamy as a snack when your're running about. Goat's cheese is one of my desert island foods and the combination of creamy cheese, pesto and tomato gives an explosion of flavour. If you're making my kale, feta and red pepper filo pie (page 158) you can use the leftover pastry and filling to make these wonderful little gems.

3 tbsp olive oil, plus extra for brushing

4 onions, thinly sliced

6 cloves garlic, crushed

450g cherry tomatoes, halved

4 tbsp pesto, homemade (page 107) or shop-bought

200g goat's cheese, crumbled

3 large sheets filo pastry

Sea salt and freshly ground black pepper

Preheat the oven to 180°C/160°C fan/350°F/Gas mark 4 and line a 12-hole muffin tray with pieces of foil.

Heat the olive oil in a frying pan over a medium heat. Add the onions and sauté for 12–15 minutes until soft and golden. Add the garlic and fry for a further 30 seconds until aromatic. Transfer to a bowl and stir in the tomatoes, pesto, and most of the goat's cheese, then season with salt and pepper to taste.

Place the filo sheets on a work surface and, working quickly, brush each sheet with olive oil. Cut each sheet into 12 squares (covering the filo squares with a clean, damp cloth to prevent them drying out while you cut the rest), then gently press 3 squares into each hole to create the tart shells.

Spoon the tomato mixture into the shells, topping each tart with the remaining goat's cheese. Bake in the oven for about 15 minutes, until the filo is crisp and a deep golden colour. Remove from the oven and serve immediately with a fresh, green salad.

SALMON FISHCAKES

MAKES 14 FISHCAKES
(SERVES 4-6)

I usually find fishcakes rather heavy on potato, so the idea here was to create one that was more about the fish but still held together in a perfect little patty. These are great stacked high on a plate, with mayo alongside, for your guests to grab at will. Sweet potato makes them more nutritious than your average fishcake and these will taste better than the shop-bought variety. The fishcake mixture can be made ahead of time, and kept in the fridge (for up to a day ahead) or in the freezer once cooked and cooled.

200g sweet potatoes, peeled and cut into small chunks

1 large egg

600g hot smoked salmon fillets (fresh or canned), skin removed and flesh flaked

60g white spelt or rice flour, plus extra for dusting

2 spring onions, finely chopped

1 tsp sweet smoked paprika

2 tsp wholegrain mustard

Grated zest of 1 unwaxed lemon, then cut into wedges to serve

20g fresh dill, leaves stripped from the stalk and finely chopped

20g fresh flat-leaf parsley leaves, stalks removed and leaves finely chopped, plus extra to serve

1 tbsp olive oil

Sea salt and freshly ground black pepper

Mayonnaise, to serve

Place the sweet potato chunks in a large saucepan, cover with water and bring to the boil over a high heat. Reduce the heat to medium and simmer for about 15 minutes, or until they are tender when pierced with a sharp knife. Drain and return to the dry pan to dry out completely in the residual heat, then mash the sweet potato thoroughly, making sure there are no lumps.

Whisk the egg in a large bowl, then add the mashed sweet potato and the flaked smoked salmon. (If using canned salmon, make sure it is well drained of liquid.) Add the remaining ingredients (except the oil, extra parsley and lemon wedges) and gently, but thoroughly, stir to combine. Season with salt and pepper, to taste.

Divide the mixture into 14 portions. Shape each portion into a ball with your hands, then flatten into neat round fishcakes. Lay them on a clean board and transfer to the fridge for 5 minutes.

Heat the olive oil in a large frying pan over a medium heat. Gently place some of the fishcakes in the pan (you will need to cook them in batches), and fry for 4 minutes on each side, until golden. Keep warm while you cook the remaining fishcakes, then serve immediately scattered with the remaining parsley, mayonnaise, lemon wedges and a green salad if you like.

TAMARI
CHICKEN
DRUMSTICKS
WITH POMEGRANATE SEEDS

SERVES 6

We love to have a good old gathering at our house, and making a huge dish of these always goes down well. In fact we always end up wishing we had made more as they go so quickly. Marinate overnight so on the day they're full of flavour and ready to cook. I don't eat chicken but love making these for other hungry faces. The pomegranate provides a sweet crunch and looks beautiful.

4 tbsp tamari or soy sauce

2 tbsp maple syrup

2 tsp toasted sesame oil

1 tbsp olive oil

6 cloves garlic, crushed

4cm piece of root ginger, peeled and finely grated

12 chicken drumsticks

Small handful of fresh flat-leaf parsley leaves, roughly chopped

3 tbsp pomegranate seeds

Combine the tamari or soy sauce, maple syrup, sesame oil, olive oil, garlic and ginger in a large bowl. Slash the skin of each drumstick three times, add them to the bowl, coat with the marinade, cover and chill for at least 6 hours, or overnight.

When ready to cook, preheat the oven to 200°C/180°C fan/400°F/Gas mark 6.

Transfer the marinated chicken and all the marinade to a large baking tray. Roast for 35–40 minutes, turning the drumsticks occasionally, until the chicken is cooked through and the skin is slightly blistered and golden.

Transfer the drumsticks to a serving dish, scatter over the parsley and pomegranate seeds and serve immediately.

FRIED QUINOA BALLS

SERVES 4–6 (MAKES APPROXIMATELY 30)

This is a lovely twist on the risotto ball, and is a great way to use up leftover quinoa. You can make a big batch and serve them on a sharing plate for everyone to tuck into. My mum is a particularly huge fan of these when she comes over for dinner. They're light and full of flavour, and a game-changer for the quinoa nay-sayers out there.

Extra virgin olive oil, for frying and drizzling

1 onion, finely chopped

4 cloves garlic, crushed

200g cooked quinoa (see technique on page 22), at room temperature

4 eggs, beaten

100g feta, crumbled

¼ tsp sea salt

20g fresh basil leaves, finely chopped

Grated zest of 1 unwaxed lemon

120g spelt breadcrumbs (gluten-free if you prefer)

Parmesan cheese, grated, to serve

A few parsley leaves, to serve

Heat 1 tablespoon olive oil in a frying pan over a medium heat. Add the onion and sauté for 5 minutes until softened, then add the garlic and fry for a further minute until aromatic, taking care not to let it burn. Transfer the onion and garlic to a mixing bowl.

Add the cooked quinoa to the bowl with the eggs, feta, salt, basil, lemon zest and breadcrumbs and mix gently to combine. Set aside for 10 minutes, until the breadcrumbs have absorbed most of the liquid then, using your hands, shape the mixture into about 30 3cm balls. Slightly flatten the balls and lay them on a board.

Heat 3 tablespoons of oil in a large frying pan over a low heat. When hot, carefully add the balls (in batches if necessary) and fry for 10 minutes, turning them occasionally, until crisp and a deep golden colour.

Remove from the pan and serve immediately with Parmesan shavings and parsley leaves scattered over, and a little drizzle of extra virgin olive oil.

AUBERGINE, PUY LENTIL & CHERRY TOMATO SALAD

SERVES 4

I adore aubergines. They are packed with flavour and have a wonderfully moreish texture. This is a truly tasty and filling, yet simple, salad that is full of goodness in every way. The lentils make a great base for this dish and sit prettily under the juicy aubergine. Serve it on a big plate for your friends or family to dig into.

Olive oil, for frying and brushing

1 yellow or white onion, finely chopped

4 garlic cloves, finely chopped

300g puy lentils, rinsed and drained

1 litre vegetable stock (page 173) or make it with good quality bouillon powder

3 aubergines, cut into 2cm-thick round slices

1 tbsp honey

3 tbsp extra virgin olive oil

Grated zest of 1 unwaxed lemon

1 tbsp red wine vinegar

1 tbsp soy sauce

1 small red onion, halved and thinly sliced

14 cherry tomatoes, halved

Large handful of fresh flat-leaf parsley leaves

100g goat's cheese, sliced (optional)

Sea salt and freshly ground black pepper

Heat 2 tablespoons of the olive oil in a large saucepan (with a lid) over a medium heat. Add the yellow or white onion and sauté gently for 5 minutes until soft and translucent. Add the garlic and fry for a further minute, then add the lentils and vegetable stock. Bring to the boil, then reduce to a simmer, cover and cook for about 25 minutes or until the lentils are tender with a little bite, and have absorbed the majority of the stock.

Meanwhile, use a pastry brush to coat the aubergine slices with olive oil on both sides. Heat a large dry frying pan over a medium heat, then place the aubergine slices in the pan and fry for 8–10 minutes on each side, until golden brown and soft to the touch. Transfer to a plate and season each slice with sea salt and pepper, then drizzle over the honey and 1 tablespoon of the extra virgin olive oil.

When the lentils are cooked, remove the lid and pour off any excess stock, keeping about 1 tablespoon of liquid behind, with the lentils. While they are still hot, add the lemon zest, red wine vinegar and soy sauce and the remaining 2 tablespoons of extra virgin olive oil. Add the sliced red onion, cherry tomatoes and most of the parsley. Mix thoroughly and leave to cool slightly. When ready to serve, taste and adjust the seasoning if necessary with a little more soy sauce, vinegar or extra virgin olive oil.

To serve, layer the aubergine and lentils on a large dish, and scatter over the remaining parsley and the cheese, if using.

TERIYAKI COD

SERVES 2

This is one of the quickest and yummiest dinners around, so if you're hungry and don't have much time to spare this ticks all the boxes. The cod is melt-in-the-mouth and packed with protein, while the spinach powers more great greens into your diet.

2 boneless cod fillets, skin on

1 tbsp coconut oil, melted

2 tbsp teriyaki sauce

200g spinach leaves

1 tsp toasted sesame oil

1 spring onion, finely chopped, to serve

Sesame seeds, to serve

Sea salt and freshly ground black pepper, to taste

Preheat the oven to 200°C/180°C fan/400°F/Gas mark 6.

Place the cod fillets skin side down in a baking tray, coat all over with the coconut oil and teriyaki sauce, and season with pepper. Bake in the oven for about 10 minutes, or until just cooked through.

Meanwhile, rinse the spinach under cold running water and put it straight into a dry frying pan over a high heat. Cook the spinach for 2 minutes, turning it as it wilts, then transfer it to a sieve and gently press out any remaining water. Spread it out on a plate and, while it's still hot, season with the sesame oil and a pinch of salt and pepper.

Serve the cod alongside the spinach, with the spring onion and sesame seeds scattered over.

During the week, meals can be rushed and neglected, but come the weekend...IT'S ON!

My mum still can't get her head around having a cooked meal at lunchtime, apart from a cracking Sunday lunch. If you don't work at the weekend you'll know what a luxury a long lunch is. It's a chance to sit down and chat, and truly enjoy what you're putting in your body. I'm not talking about eating a mountain of stodge that'll sit like a brick in your stomach all afternoon, easing you into a sofa coma. I'm talking about delicious goodness that tastes divine.

The long-held British tradition of a Sunday lunch is still set in most people's DNA, whether it's a family pub outing, or a regular trip to your nan's for her much-loved gravy. The ethos of a Sunday sit-down lunch doesn't have to change one bit, but the menu can. You can still have your hearty British traditions but without the heavy bloated feeling afterwards.

Before I started to eat fish in my mid-twenties I was a bored vegetarian who was dished out six more roast spuds as a meat substitute. Vegetarian gravy was rarely on offer, so I was left with a rather bland and dry-looking plate of food. As more vegetarian and pescetarians emerge, the more options there are.

I've created the recipes in this chapter with a leisurely Saturday or Sunday lunch in mind but, of course, they can be enjoyed any time. There are a couple of meaty options, as the kids love to indulge in a classic spag bol or my husband's famous roast chicken, and many gorgeous meals that will feel light and energising yet comforting and homely. Some are really great meals to make as a family, too. We love to get the kids involved in helping out. It's fun for them and they learn about what they're eating, too. These dishes work well for big groups, or all the family, but equally for solo dining.

Weekend eating can be a great way of packing in as much veg as you can, too. In our busy lives it's important we give our bodies the right fuel and pump it with the vitamins and nutrients it needs to function as well as it can. So rather than slumping on the sofa after a heavy roast, it's time to fill up on goodness then make the most of your weekend.

Weekend Classics

VEGGIE SHEPHERD'S PIE

SERVES 6–8

I dedicate this recipe to my mother, who stopped eating meat the same day as me all those years ago. This is a great dish to serve up to those suspicious of vegetarian food, as it feels hearty and comforting, much like the classic version. As well as the filling being packed with veg, the mash topping is made from cauliflower so you get even more veg than you bargained for, and a much lighter eating experience, too.

For the cauliflower mash:

4 tbsp olive oil

2 heads of cauliflower, cut into small florets

6 tbsp water

4 cloves garlic, crushed

2 tbsp coconut cream, taken from the top of a can of full-fat coconut milk (or buy canned coconut cream)

1 tbsp grated Parmesan cheese, plus extra for sprinkling

Sea salt and freshly ground black pepper

For the filling:

1 tbsp olive or coconut oil

1 onion, finely chopped

5 carrots, diced

4 cloves garlic, crushed

200ml vegetable stock (page 173) or good quality bouillon powder

400g can green or brown lentils, drained and rinsed

400g can haricot beans, drained and rinsed

Large handful of kale, tough stems removed and leaves finely chopped

3 tbsp pesto, shop-bought or homemade (page 107)

1½ tsp ground cumin

2 tsp cornflour

Sea salt and freshly ground black pepper

Preheat the oven to 200°C/180°C fan/400°F/Gas mark 6.

To make the cauliflower mash, heat the oil in a large saucepan (with a lid) over a medium–high heat. Add the cauliflower and fry for 2 minutes. Reduce the heat to low, add the water, cover and steam for 15–20 minutes, or until tender when pierced with a sharp knife. Add the garlic and sauté for 1–2 minutes until fragrant, taking care not to let it burn, then remove from the heat and transfer the cauliflower and garlic to the bowl of a food processor with the coconut cream and Parmesan, and blitz until completely smooth. Season generously with salt and pepper, transfer to a bowl, cover and set aside.

While the cauliflower is steaming, start making the filling. Heat the oil in a separate saucepan (with a lid) over a medium heat. Add the onion and carrot and sauté for 5 minutes, then add the garlic and fry for a further minute until fragrant. Add the stock, lentils, beans and kale, cover, bring to the boil, then reduce the temperature to low and simmer gently for 5 minutes. Stir in the pesto and cumin and season well with salt and pepper. Lightly mash the mixture, just to break open some of the beans, then add the cornflour and mix thoroughly over the heat, until the mixture is thick and holding together. Taste, and if necessary, adjust the seasoning with a little more salt and pepper.

Ladle the filling mixture into a 24 x 18cm ovenproof dish, spread over the cauliflower mash and smooth it out. Sprinkle with more grated Parmesan and pepper, then bake for 25 minutes or until golden.

VEGETABLE & MOZZARELLA BAKE

SERVES 6–8

My perfect cosy night in always features this dish, as it feels like a warm hug on a cold night. The layers of veggies offer up your daily dose of vitamins and the mozzarella is a good source of protein, with the added bonus of making this a decadently creamy bake.

1 tbsp coconut or olive oil, plus extra for greasing and drizzling

1 onion, finely chopped

3 cloves garlic, crushed

4 beef tomatoes, chopped

1 tsp ground cumin

2 tsp maple syrup

1 tsp tamari or soy sauce

1 medium sweet potato, peeled and thinly sliced lengthways

2 large balls of buffalo mozzarella, drained

2 courgettes, thinly sliced lengthways

½ aubergine, thinly sliced lengthways

Parmesan cheese, for grating

Leaves stripped from 4 sprigs of fresh thyme

Sea salt and freshly ground black pepper

Preheat the oven to 200°C/180°C fan/400°F/Gas mark 6 and grease a 22 x 18cm ovenproof dish.

Heat the oil in a large saucepan (with a lid) over a medium heat. Add the onion and sauté for 5 minutes until translucent, then add the garlic and fry for a further minute. Add the chopped tomatoes, cumin, maple syrup and tamari or soy sauce, then cover and bring to the boil. Reduce the heat to low and simmer for 10 minutes. Remove from the heat, season to taste with salt and pepper and set aside.

Cover the base of the ovenproof dish with the sweet potato slices, season with a pinch of salt and pepper and drizzle with a little olive oil. Cover with a third of the tomato sauce and tear a third of the mozzarella on top. Lay half of the courgette slices over the torn mozzarella and tomato sauce, season again with salt and pepper and drizzle with a little olive oil, then add another third of the tomato sauce and mozzarella. Layer the aubergine slices on top, season again, then add the remaining tomato sauce. Top with a layer of the remaining courgette, season again, tear over the remaining mozzarella and grate over a thin layer of Parmesan. Finally, scatter over the thyme leaves.

Bake in the oven for 40–45 minutes until the top is bubbling and golden. Serve immediately, with a green salad on the side.

NUTTY KALE SIDE SALAD

SERVES 4 AS A SIDE
DISH OR 2 AS A
LIGHT LUNCH

I eat this nearly every day as I can't get enough of the flavour combination. I love eating kale as it's full of iron, which non-meat-eaters have to work a bit harder to get. As well as being a great side dish for a weekend lunch, it's also amazing as a light weekday lunch with an add-on of chorizo, tomatoes or broccoli, or almost anything you have in your fridge. This is definitely a tasty way of getting those greens in your system.

1 tbsp tahini

1 tbsp almond butter (page 30 or shop-bought)

5 tbsp olive oil

Grated zest of 1 unwaxed lemon and 1 tbsp juice

200g kale, tough stems removed and leaves chopped

50g toasted flaked almonds

Sea salt and freshly ground black pepper

Combine the tahini, almond butter, 2 tablespoons of the olive oil, the lemon zest and juice and a good pinch of salt and pepper in a bowl.

Heat the remaining olive oil in a frying pan over a high heat. Once hot, add the kale leaves and flash-fry for 1 minute, turning them constantly, until the kale is vibrant green and very slightly crispy on the edges. Remove from the heat and season with a pinch of salt.

Transfer to a serving dish, drizzle over the tahini and almond butter sauce, scatter over the flaked almonds and serve immediately.

SWEET POTATO FRIES

SERVES 4

These fries won't leave you feeling like the inside of a chip pan, and they are far more nutritious and flavourful than regular potato chips. They're perfect tipped into a large sharing bowl for your friends and family to descend into.

2 large sweet potatoes (about 750g), washed and cut into 1.5cm-thick chips

3 tbsp olive oil or coconut oil, melted

1 tsp sea salt

½ tsp freshly ground black pepper

1 tsp ground cumin

1 tsp sweet smoked paprika (optional)

Preheat the oven to 220°C/200°C fan/450°F/Gas mark 8 and line 2 baking sheets with baking parchment.

Place the sweet potato chips in a large bowl and combine with the remaining ingredients until evenly coated.

Divide the fries in a single layer between the 2 lined trays, making sure the trays are not too crowded, otherwise the chips will steam. Roast in the oven for 25 minutes until crisp and golden, turning them halfway through. Remove and serve immediately.

KALE, FETA & RED PEPPER FILO PIE

SERVES 6

We usually associate the word 'pie' with a heap of stodge and a lazy feeling to follow. I've never been a huge fan of them, probably because of scoffing a dodgy one from a petrol station once. This delightful version is much less heavy on the gut than your typical pie, and is full of flavour. Filo is a very light pastry so the main event really is the filling, stuffed with vitamins and protein from the veg and feta.

200g kale, rinsed and dried, tough stems removed and leaves chopped into small pieces

2 tbsp olive oil, plus extra for brushing

2 tbsp balsamic vinegar

4 cloves garlic, crushed

2 eggs, beaten

350g feta, crumbled

Grated zest of 1 unwaxed lemon

3 tbsp pine nuts

150g roasted red peppers from a jar, drained and cut into thin strips

8 large sheets filo pastry

1 tbsp Dijon mustard

Sea salt and freshly ground black pepper

Preheat the oven to 190°C/170°C fan/375°F/Gas mark 5.

Put the kale leaves in a large bowl with the olive oil and balsamic vinegar. Using your hands, massage the oil and vinegar into the leaves until they are all evenly coated and slightly softened. Add the remaining ingredients (apart from the filo and mustard), plus a generous pinch or two of pepper and a small pinch of salt, taking care not to add too much as the feta is already salty. Mix everything together until thoroughly combined.

Working quickly, brush 7 of the filo pastry sheets with olive oil and use them to line a 24 x 18cm ovenproof dish, laying them in alternating directions so that by the time you've laid all the sheets, you have an overhang of filo pastry the entire way round the dish. Keep the remaining filo sheet covered with a damp tea towel to prevent it drying out.

Spread the mustard on the base of the filo shell, then add the kale mixture, pressing it gently into the dish. Cut the remaining filo sheet in half, brush the two halves with oil then lay them on top of the pie, crumpling the sheets slightly for texture. Fold up the overhanging sheets of filo, scrunching them around the pie to create a border.

Bake in the oven for 30–35 minutes, or until the filling has set and the filo is a deep golden colour and crisp to the touch. If it is browning too quickly towards the end of cooking, cover the pie loosely with foil.

Remove from the oven and leave to cool for 10 minutes, then serve in wedges with a light green salad.

JESSE'S ROAST CHICKEN

SERVES 6

This is Jesse's speciality. We often have family over on a Sunday and they all look forward to tucking into this dish. Although I don't eat chicken, my family rave about the flavours from the herbs and the hint of lemon that creeps through. It's a classic that makes a weekend that bit more special. Serve this up with any veg you desire. It goes particularly well with maple-glazed carrots (page 165), pan-fried broccoli with chilli flakes and crispy garlic (page 165) and pan-fried courgette with cumin and goat's cheese (page 166).

1.8kg free-range chicken

20g fresh basil, stalks removed, leaves finely chopped

10g fresh tarragon, stalks removed, leaves finely chopped

4 tbsp olive oil

1 tsp sea salt

½ tsp freshly ground black pepper

1 lemon

3 red onions, halved

1 bulb of garlic, separated into cloves (no need to peel)

Remove the chicken from the fridge 30 minutes before cooking. Preheat the oven to 220°C/200°C fan/425°F/ Gas mark 7.

Combine the chopped herbs with 3 tablespoons of the olive oil, and the salt and pepper. Place the chicken in a large roasting dish and coat it thoroughly with the herby oil, making sure it gets into all the nooks and crannies.

Stab the lemon a few times with a sharp knife or fork, and place it in the cavity of the bird. Toss the onion halves and garlic cloves in the remaining oil, season well with salt and pepper, and leave to one side.

Put the roasting dish in the preheated oven, immediately turn the temperature down to 200°C/180°C fan/400°F/ Gas mark 6, and roast the chicken for 1 hour, basting it halfway through with its own cooking juices, then add the onion and garlic cloves to the dish and roast for a further 30 minutes.

While the chicken is cooking, prepare your chosen accompaniments.

Once the chicken is cooked, remove it from the oven, cover with foil and leave to rest for 15–20 minutes. Once rested, serve the chicken on a board or platter with the onion and garlic surrounding it.

MAPLE-GLAZED CARROTS

SERVES 4

Erase the memory of your nan's slightly over-boiled, flavourless carrots on a Sunday and get ready for the real deal. These are oozing with flavour and crunch and are the perfect accompaniment to any weekend dish. I love to serve heaps of them in a large bowl so everyone can help themselves.

2 tbsp coconut oil

4 tbsp maple syrup or honey

2 tsp sea salt

2 cinnamon sticks

300ml water

8 medium carrots, cut into 1 x 6cm batons

Small handful of fresh flat-leaf parsley or thyme leaves, to serve

Put the coconut oil, maple syrup or honey, salt, cinnamon sticks and water in a saucepan (with a lid) and bring to the boil. Add the carrot batons, cover and bring back to the boil for 1 minute. Remove the lid, reduce the heat and simmer gently for 12–15 minutes, until a sharp knife glides easily into the carrots.

Serve the carrots with a little of the cooking liquid drizzled over and the herbs scattered on top.

PAN-FRIED BROCCOLI

WITH CHILLI FLAKES & CRISPY GARLIC

SERVES 4–6

I can eat ridiculous quantities of this stuff. Cooking the broccoli like this enhances all its natural flavour and is so much nicer than boiling it. This cruciferous veg is still up there as one of the healthiest around so you can up your vitamin C and K intake by including it in your diet.

2 tbsp coconut or olive oil

3 cloves garlic, thinly sliced

400g head of broccoli, broken into small florets, stalk discarded

4 tbsp water

½ tsp dried chilli flakes

Sea salt and freshly ground black pepper

Extra virgin olive oil, for drizzling

Heat the oil in a large saucepan (with a lid) over a medium heat. Add the garlic and fry for 1–2 minutes, stirring constantly, until the garlic is crisp, golden and fragrant. Watch it carefully, as it burns quickly. Transfer the garlic to a bowl, reserving the oil in the pan.

Add the broccoli florets and water to the pan, increase the heat to high, cover and let the broccoli steam for 2 minutes. Remove the lid and fry for a further minute, until the broccoli is vibrant green and tender, but still retains some bite. Toss in the chilli flakes and season with salt and pepper to taste. Transfer to a serving dish, scatter over the fried garlic and drizzle with extra virgin olive oil.

PAN-FRIED COURGETTE

WITH CUMIN & GOAT'S CHEESE

This is inspired by my first trip to the States at the age of 17, when I met the American side of my family for the first time. As soon as I landed I was whisked to a diner (another first) and had cherry cola and fried zucchini. It wasn't until the dish arrived that I realised zucchini was courgette! This is such a moreish side dish and is a great way to glam up the humble vegetable.

3 tbsp olive oil

2 courgettes, cut into ½cm-thick rounds

1 tsp cumin seeds

3 cloves garlic, crushed

80g goat's cheese

Sea salt and freshly ground black pepper

Heat the oil in a large saucepan over a medium heat. Add the courgette rounds and cumin seeds and season with a good pinch of salt and pepper. Fry for 3 minutes, then add the garlic and continue to fry for a further minute until the garlic is aromatic and the courgette is golden and tender.

Transfer to a serving dish, crumble over the goat's cheese, season with another pinch of pepper and serve immediately.

SPAGHETTI BOLOGNESE

SERVES 6

This dish is another winner with the kids. My son Rex normally isn't too keen on red meat but will scoff this by the shovel-load. It takes a bit of time to cook but after a little prep, it'll just simmer away and you can get on with other things. It also freezes very well, so it's worth making double the quantity to freeze half for another day. I use a combination of minced pork and beef, but it could be made with just one or the other, if you prefer.

2 tbsp olive oil

1 onion, finely chopped

1 stick celery, finely chopped

1 carrot, finely chopped

3 cloves garlic, crushed

Good pinch of ground or freshly grated nutmeg

200g minced pork

250g minced beef

250ml chicken stock

400g can chopped tomatoes

25 cherry tomatoes, halved

450g spaghetti

Sea salt and freshly ground black pepper

Parmesan cheese, grated, to serve

Heat the oil in a large saucepan over a medium heat. Add the onion, celery and carrot and sauté gently for 5 minutes, stirring occasionally until they start to soften and the onions are translucent. Add the garlic and nutmeg and fry for a further 2 minutes, taking care not to let the garlic burn.

Add the minced pork and beef, 1 teaspoon of salt and a good grind of pepper. Fry for about 5 minutes, breaking up any lumps of mince with a wooden spoon, until the meat is no longer pink and is just beginning to brown. Increase the heat to high, add the stock and let it bubble and reduce for 3 minutes, then stir in the canned and fresh tomatoes, reduce the heat to the lowest setting and simmer very gently for at least 1 hour, stirring from time to time to prevent the bolognese from catching on the bottom of the pan. If you prefer a thicker sauce, cook for a further 30 minutes to reduce it further. Taste and adjust the seasoning if necessary with a little more salt and pepper.

Ten minutes before the end of the cooking time, cook the spaghetti according to the packet instructions. Drain the spaghetti and add it to the pan of bolognese, stirring well to combine. Serve in deep bowls, with grated Parmesan on top.

TOFU CASSEROLE

SERVES 4-6

Tofu doesn't have the best reputation, but this dish is a game-changer. It has bags of flavour, and is comforting and substantial yet virtuous. Tofu contains loads of protein, and the veg provide tons of nutrients. You need to prepare the marinated tofu the night before (page 65), but after that you're almost there. I love cooking a big casserole, as everyone can help themselves and any leftovers can be mopped up with bread. Heaven.

2 tbsp coconut oil

1 leek, trimmed, halved lengthways and thinly sliced

3cm piece of root ginger, peeled and finely grated

2 cloves garlic, crushed

400g can chopped tomatoes

100ml full-fat coconut milk

2 tsp honey or maple syrup

400g can chickpeas, drained and rinsed

200g cooked or canned lentils, drained and rinsed

400g cherry tomatoes, halved

1 quantity of marinated tofu (page 65)

Small handful of fresh flat-leaf parsley, leaves finely chopped

Extra virgin olive oil, for drizzling

Sea salt and freshly ground black pepper

8 sprigs of thyme

60g feta cheese, to garnish (optional)

Preheat the oven to 200°C/180°C fan/400°F/Gas mark 6.

Heat the coconut oil in a large saucepan (with a lid) over a medium heat. Add the leek and ginger and season with a pinch of salt and pepper. Sauté for 8–10 minutes until the leeks are tender, then add the garlic and fry for a further 30 seconds until aromatic. Add the canned tomatoes, coconut milk, honey or maple syrup, chickpeas and lentils. Cover, bring to the boil, then reduce the heat and simmer for 5 minutes. Add the cherry tomatoes, marinated tofu and most of the parsley, and stir to combine. Taste and adjust the seasoning if necessary, then transfer the mixture to a 22 x 16cm ovenproof dish. Drizzle over a little oil, place the thyme sprigs on top and bake for 20 minutes.

Scatter with the remaining parsley, and crumble over the feta, if you are using it.

QUICK VEGETABLE STOCK

MAKES ABOUT 1 LITRE

Homemade stock is a fantastic foundation to so many delicious, nourishing dishes, such as my lentil, haricot and veg soup (page 61). Used in stews, broths and casseroles, it adds warmth and depth of flavour, which is why I often use it to cook quinoa. I try to make a double batch so that I have a handy stash in the freezer, where it will keep for up to 3 months.

2 carrots, halved

1 onion, halved (no need to peel)

½ small garlic bulb, unpeeled and sliced in half

2 sticks celery, including leaves, halved

1 tsp black peppercorns

3 bay leaves

Large handful of fresh parsley, stalks and leaves

Place all the ingredients in a saucepan and cover with 1.2 litres of cold water. Bring to a rolling boil and keep at boiling point for 30 minutes. Remove from the heat, and strain the stock through a sieve into a heatproof container. The stock can be used immediately or, once cool, it can be kept in the fridge for 3–4 days, or frozen for up to 3 months.

For me, baking is a form of meditation. I couldn't be happier than when I'm in cake mode. I go into a trance-like state where I zone out from the surrounding noise to be transported to a place where only cake exists.

I've been like this for a long time. My first memory of baking is with my nan, Ruby. I would go to her house at the weekend and we would crack on with the jam tarts. They were sickly sweet, slightly burnt and completely delicious.

When I moved out of home at the age of 19, baking became a post-work hobby. It was a way to wind down after a manic day travelling around, with scripts to learn, TV shows to film and general chaos. Making cakes became a way to instantly bring myself back down to earth and has always had a slightly romantic association, too. In my memory, I'm in the little kitchen of my first flat, the rain is pouring outside, the radio is on in the background, and everything smells of sweet vanilla. As you can tell, I'm awfully nostalgic about cake.

My Aunty Karen is a cake wizard. She has, over the years, made cakes that resemble a VW bug car, Snow White's seven dwarves in a bed, and a glittery unicorn (and the list goes on). She's unstoppable. My cakes tend to take on a more rustic look, but they do taste delicious. If someone is coming over for tea or a quick hello, my baking reflex kicks in, and there will ALWAYS be cake. This has set quite a precedent, however, so when I haven't had a chance to bake my guests look genuinely disgruntled. Some (cough cough . . . Reggie Yates) will even specify which type of cake they would like on their arrival. I of course love this and wouldn't have it any other way!

As you'll know, I've said goodbye to refined sugar and only have it as a treat now and then. This doesn't have to mean dry, worthy-looking cakes though. Here you'll find recipes that will make your mouth water just by looking at them, but won't leave you shaking from a sugar rush or suffering a crash 30 minutes after eating them. They're light, dreamy and delicious.

You would never know that these cakes and bakes were any different to standard sugar-packed ones, but your insides, mood and energy levels most definitely will. It's the true cheat – you are simply having your cake and eating it!

The Bakery

EARL GREY BISCUITS

MAKES 12–14 BISCUITS

My mum LOVES tea. She must drink ten-plus cups a day, so these aromatic biscuits are dedicated to her and her habit. They have a unique flavour that'll tingle your taste buds and be the perfect partner for your cuppa.

60g coconut palm sugar

60g coconut oil

2½ tsp Earl Grey tea leaves, finely ground in a pestle and mortar or spice grinder

110g white spelt flour, sifted

½ tsp baking powder

Pinch of fine sea salt

Finely grated zest of 1 unwaxed lemon

¾ tsp vanilla extract

Preheat the oven to 180°C/160°C fan/350°F/Gas mark 4 and line 2 baking trays with baking parchment.

Place the coconut palm sugar and coconut oil in a bowl and beat with a wooden spoon until very well incorporated and creamy.

Put the ground tea leaves in a separate bowl with the flour, baking powder, salt and lemon zest.

Add the flour mixture to the sugar and coconut oil mixture and thoroughly combine. Once everything is incorporated, drizzle over the vanilla extract and use your hands to bring the mixture into a ball. It may seem a little dry at first, but keep on kneading and compressing the dough with your hands until it all comes together. If, after a minute or two, it is not coming together, add 1–2 drops of water and continue kneading. Don't be tempted to add the water too early though, as the flour needs time to absorb the moisture as you knead.

Take a heaped teaspoon of the dough and roll it into a ball. Place on a baking tray and flatten out gently into a neat ¾cm-thick, round biscuit shape. Continue with the remaining dough, leaving a 2–3cm gap between each biscuit. Place both trays in the oven for 8 minutes, until the biscuits are a shade darker and rough textured on top. They burn easily, so be sure to time them. Remove from the oven, leave to cool for 10 minutes then carefully transfer to a wire rack to cool completely. They will be soft at first, but will become crunchy as they cool.

These keep well for up to 5 days stored in an airtight container.

CHERRY BERRY SPONGE CAKE

SERVES 10–12

Making big, beautiful cakes is one of my favourite pastimes. Eating them is my ULTIMATE favourite. I find the whole process cathartic, from the careful layering to the fantasy-filled decorations on top. This cake is as pretty as a peach and you can really go to town on the decorations if it's for a special occasion – edible glitter goes down a storm!

For the icing:

2 x 400ml cans full-fat coconut milk, chilled

3½ tbsp set honey

1½ tbsp cornflour

½ tsp vanilla extract

2 tbsp coconut oil, melted

Pinch of sea salt

For the sponge:

225g coconut palm sugar

200g coconut oil, plus extra for greasing

4 eggs, beaten

2 tbsp almond milk (page 50 or shop-bought), rice milk or dairy milk

1 tsp vanilla extract

225g white spelt flour, sifted

2 tsp baking powder

1 tsp bicarbonate of soda

¼ tsp fine sea salt

For the topping:

150g cherries, strawberries and blueberries

Edible glitter and fresh flowers, to decorate (optional)

Preheat the oven to 180°C/160°C fan/350°F/Gas mark 4. Grease two 18cm springform round cake tins and line the bases with baking parchment.

To make the icing, remove the cans of coconut milk from the fridge without shaking them. Remove the lids and carefully scoop out the very firm, set coconut cream at the top, leaving the coconut water in the cans (don't throw the water away – use it to make soups, curries, porridge or smoothies). Add the thick coconut cream to the bowl of a food processor with the remaining icing ingredients and blitz until completely smooth. Transfer to a bowl, cover and chill for at least 1 hour to set.

To make the sponge, place the coconut palm sugar and coconut oil in a bowl and cream together until light and well incorporated. Beat in the eggs a little at a time, followed by the milk and vanilla, then fold in the flour, baking powder, bicarbonate of soda and salt until well combined. Divide the mixture between the prepared cake tins and bake in the oven for about 25 minutes, or until a skewer inserted into the centre of the cakes comes out fairly clean. Remove the cakes from the oven and leave to cool for 10 minutes, then carefully turn them out on to a wire rack to cool completely.

Once the cakes are completely cool, spread one cake with half of the icing, then place the second cake on top of the first and ice again. Decorate the top of the cake with the cherries, berries, edible glitter and flowers, if you like.

RONNIE'S FRUIT CAKE

SERVES 10–12

My father-in-law loves a fruit cake so this recipe is for him. It's a classic with a healthy twist. The fruit is soaked in tea overnight so has a rich and full-bodied flavour. I love to make this cake and give it to people as a gift wrapped in parchment and a ribbon.

200g sultanas
200g currants
350ml cold black or chai tea
250g white spelt flour, sifted
200g coconut palm sugar
½ tsp mixed spice
½ tsp ground cinnamon
Grated zest of 1 unwaxed lemon
2 tsp baking powder
2 eggs, beaten
Vegetable oil, for greasing

Place the sultanas and currants in a bowl, cover with the cold tea, and leave to steep overnight, covered, at room temperature.

The next day, preheat the oven to 200°C/180°C fan/400°F/Gas mark 6. Grease a 1kg (10 x 20cm) loaf tin and line the base and sides with baking parchment.

Add the remaining ingredients to a bowl together with the soaked sultanas and currants, and the liquid they were steeped in. Mix together until thoroughly combined.

Pour the mixture into the prepared loaf tin and bake in the oven for 1 hour 30 minutes, or until a skewer inserted into the middle of the cake comes out clean. If it looks like the top of the cake is going to burn at any point during baking, cover with foil.

Remove the cake from the oven and leave it to cool for 10 minutes before turning it out on to a wire rack to cool completely.

Serve cut into slices with coconut oil or butter, or just as it is, with a cup of tea of course! It will keep well in an airtight container for up to a week.

SPICED OATMEAL BISCUITS

MAKES 12–14 BISCUITS

My good friend Ali gave me a challenge to make her favourite childhood biscuits but without any nasty ingredients – these are the result! They're warm and spicy, packed full of crunch and lovely with a cuppa. These are fantastic too for any vegan visitors.

60g coconut palm sugar
60g coconut oil
50g rolled porridge oats or coarse oatmeal
2 tsp mixed spice
60g white spelt flour, sifted
½ tsp baking powder
Pinch of sea salt
½ tsp vanilla extract

Preheat the oven to 180°C/160°C fan/350°F/Gas mark 4 and line 2 baking trays with baking parchment.

Place the coconut sugar and oil in a bowl and beat with a wooden spoon until very well incorporated and creamy.

If using porridge oats, place them in the bowl of a food processor and blitz for a few seconds until they have a coarse oatmeal texture. Add the ground oats or oatmeal to a bowl and combine with the mixed spice, flour, baking powder and salt.

Add the flour mixture to the sugar and coconut oil mixture and thoroughly combine. Once everything is incorporated, drizzle over the vanilla extract and use your hands to form the mixture into a ball. It may seem a little dry at first, but keep on compressing the dough with your hands until it all comes together. If, after a minute or two, it is not coming together, add 1–2 drops of water and continue kneading. Don't be tempted to add the water too early though!

Take a heaped teaspoon of the dough and roll it into a ball. Place on a baking tray and flatten out gently into a neat ¾cm-thick, round biscuit shape. Continue with the remaining dough, leaving a 2–3cm gap between each biscuit. Place both trays in the oven for 8–9 minutes, until the biscuits are a shade darker and rough textured on top. They burn easily, so be sure to time them. Remove from the oven, leave to cool for 10 minutes then carefully transfer to a wire rack to cool completely. They will be soft at first, but will become crunchy as they cool. Serve immediately or store in an airtight container (they will keep for up to 4 days).

DEATH BY CHOCOLATE CAKE

SERVES 12

This is the dream cake for a big occasion and one of my all-time favourites to make as a birthday treat for a friend. It looks utterly devilish but contains no refined sugar or dairy. No one will believe it is sin-free! The thickness of the cream in cans of coconut milk varies, so try out a few different brands.

For the chocolate sponge:
300g white spelt flour, sifted
100g unsweetened cocoa powder
1½ tsp bicarbonate of soda
2 tsp baking powder
½ tsp fine sea salt
2 tsp vanilla extract
350g maple syrup or honey
460ml almond milk (page 50 or shop-bought) or rice milk
150g coconut oil, melted, plus extra for greasing
1½ tsp cider vinegar

For the coconut icing:
3 x 400ml cans full-fat coconut milk, chilled overnight
5 tbsp set honey
5 tbsp unsweetened cocoa powder
1 tsp vanilla extract
Good pinch of fine sea salt

To decorate:
Handful of fresh strawberries, hulled and halved
Chocolate shards, page 204 (optional)
1 tsp icing sugar (optional)

Preheat the oven to 180°C/160°C fan/350°F/Gas mark 4. Lightly grease two 20cm springform round cake tins and line the bases with baking parchment.

To make the sponge, combine all the dry ingredients in a large mixing bowl. In a separate bowl, mix together all the wet ingredients, except the vinegar. Add the liquid mixture to the flour mixture and fold together. Stir the vinegar into the mixture, then immediately divide the mixture evenly between the prepared cake tins. Bake in the oven for 30–35 minutes, or until a skewer inserted into the centre of the cakes comes out fairly clean. Remove the cakes from the oven and leave to cool for 10 minutes, then carefully turn them out on to a wire rack to cool completely.

To make the icing, remove the cans of coconut milk from the fridge without shaking them. Remove the lids and carefully scoop out the very firm, set coconut cream at the top, leaving the coconut water in the cans (don't throw the water away – use it to make soups, curries, porridge or smoothies). Add the thick coconut cream to the bowl of a food processor, add the set honey, cocoa powder, vanilla extract and salt, and blitz until completely smooth. Transfer to a bowl, cover and chill for at least 30 minutes.

Once the cakes are completely cool (this is important, otherwise the icing will melt), ice both layers to create a sandwich.

Decorate the top with the strawberries, and if you wish, chocolate shards and a light dusting of icing sugar.

BANANA BREAD

SERVES 8–10

This recipe is an ode to my dear husband Jesse, who would happily live off banana bread if he had a choice. Every time his band rehearse, he asks if I can make them one of these to demolish during their break. Full of flavour, it's a healthy twist on the classic and a great source of slow-release energy. If you're a first-time baker, this easy recipe is a really good starting point. Eat it by the slice, spread it with your favourite topping, or bake it for a pal. It's a real crowd-pleaser.

100g coconut oil, at room temperature, plus extra for greasing

150g coconut palm sugar

2 eggs, beaten

2 very ripe bananas, peeled and mashed with a fork

3 tbsp almond milk (page 50 or shop-bought) or rice milk

150g white or wholegrain spelt flour, sifted

2½ tsp mixed spice

½ tsp fine sea salt

2 tsp baking powder

60g walnuts, roughly chopped

20g chia seeds

Preheat the oven to 180°C/160°C fan/350°F/Gas mark 4. Grease a 1kg (10 x 20cm) loaf tin and line the base and sides with baking parchment.

Place the coconut oil and the sugar in a large bowl and cream together until light and fluffy, then beat in the eggs by hand or with an electric hand-held mixer, a little at a time, followed by the mashed banana and almond or rice milk, until well combined.

Combine the remaining ingredients in a separate bowl. Gradually fold the dry ingredients into the coconut oil and sugar mixture, until it just comes together. Don't over-mix as it will make the banana bread tough.

Transfer the mixture to the lined loaf tin and bake for about 50 minutes, or until a skewer inserted into the middle of the loaf comes out clean. If the top is browning too quickly, cover it with foil. Remove from the oven and let it cool in the tin for 10 minutes, then turn it out on to a wire rack to cool completely.

The cake is best eaten the day it's made, but it will keep for up to 3 days in an airtight container and it can be frozen for up to 2 months. Serve with anything you like: coconut oil, jam or nut butter work well.

MINI CARROT, SPELT & SPICE SCONES

MAKES 8–10
MINI SCONES

I love scones, and the whole ritual of 'afternoon tea'. I wish there was a law that meant we all had to stop each afternoon for this old-school observance. These scones are packed with carrot and spelt, and are just sweet enough. I love getting more veg in my diet in any way I can, so incorporating them into bakes makes me very happy.

220g white spelt flour, sifted, plus extra for dusting
2 tsp mixed spice
1 tsp ground or freshly grated nutmeg
2 tsp baking powder
1 tsp bicarbonate of soda
½ tsp fine sea salt
200g carrots, coarsely grated
30g coconut oil, melted, plus extra to serve
2 tbsp honey or maple syrup
80g sultanas
1 egg, beaten, for brushing
Almond butter (page 30 or shop-bought) and jam, to serve

Preheat the oven to 180°C/160°C fan/350°F/Gas mark 4 and line a baking tray with baking parchment.

Place the flour, spices, baking powder, bicarbonate of soda and salt in a bowl and stir to combine.

Roughly chop the grated carrot to get rid of any long strands, then add it to the flour mixture together with the coconut oil, honey (or maple syrup) and sultanas. Combine with a spoon, then use your hands to bring the mixture all together to form a ball. It may seem a little dry at first, but keep on compressing the mixture with your hands and it will form a dough. Try to work quickly and not over-work the dough, as this will result in tough scones.

Lightly dust the work surface with flour and roll out the dough out to a thickness of about 3cm. Use a 5cm clean-edged round cutter to punch out 8–10 scones, dipping the cutter in flour as you go, before cutting, to prevent it sticking to the dough. Use up all the leftover scraps of dough, rolling it out again and punching out scones as before.

Place the scones on the lined baking tray and brush with a little beaten egg. Bake in the oven for 13–15 minutes, or until they have risen and are golden brown.

Remove from the oven and serve warm, spread with your favourite jam, almond butter and some coconut oil. They will keep for up to 2 days in an airtight container – reheat before serving.

CASHEW & APRICOT BISCUITS

MAKES 12–14 BISCUITS

These moreish, dreamy little biscuits are a favourite of my son Rex. They're great for kids as they are packed with nutritious apricots and omega-3-packed chia seeds.

60g coconut palm sugar

60g coconut oil

50g raw unsalted cashew nuts, finely chopped

50g unsulphured dried apricots, finely chopped

100g white spelt flour, sifted

½ tsp baking powder

1½ tbsp chia seeds

Pinch of sea salt

1 tsp vanilla extract

Preheat the oven to 180°C/160°C fan/350°F/Gas mark 4 and line 2 baking trays with baking parchment.

Place the coconut palm sugar and coconut oil in a bowl, and beat with a wooden spoon until very well incorporated and creamy.

Put the chopped cashews and apricots in a separate bowl, checking there aren't any large chunks, and combine with the flour, baking powder, chia seeds and salt.

Add the flour mixture to the sugar and coconut oil mixture and thoroughly combine. Once everything is incorporated, drizzle over the vanilla extract and use your hands to form the mixture into a ball. It may seem a little dry at first, but keep on kneading and compressing the dough with your hands until it all comes together. If, after a minute or two, it is not coming together, add 1–2 drops of water and continue kneading. Don't be tempted to add the water too early though, as the flour needs time to absorb the moisture as you knead.

Take a heaped teaspoon of the dough and roll it into a ball. Place on a baking tray and flatten out gently into a neat ¾cm-thick, round biscuit shape. Continue with the remaining dough, leaving a 2–3cm gap between each biscuit. Place both trays in the oven for 8–9 minutes, until the biscuits are a shade darker and rough textured on top. They burn easily, so be sure to time them. Remove from the oven, leave to cool for 10 minutes then carefully transfer to a wire rack to cool completely. They will be soft at first, but will become crunchy as they cool.

BASIC CUPCAKE

MAKES 12 CUPCAKES

I love a cheeky cupcake and these are the prettiest, most delicious of treats that are kind to your body. Regular cupcakes are crammed with sugar, leaving you in a flop shortly after eating them but these gems allow you to bypass all of that. There's also the added bonus of them being free from dairy, making them feel very light without compromising on flavour. These cakes are darker in colour than their traditional counterparts on account of the coconut palm sugar, which imparts a rich caramel flavour. Top these with some icing (pages 194-5) choosing whichever flavour takes your fancy.

125g coconut palm sugar
125g coconut oil, at room temperature
2 eggs, beaten
½ tsp vanilla extract
125g white spelt flour, sifted
2 tsp baking powder

Preheat the oven to 180°C/160°C fan/350°F/Gas mark 4 and line a 12-hole muffin tray with paper cases.

Place the coconut palm sugar and coconut oil in a bowl, and cream together with a wooden spoon or an electric hand-held whisk until light and well combined. Beat in the eggs, a little at a time, then add the vanilla extract, and fold in the flour and baking powder until combined.

Half-fill each of the paper cases with the mixture, then bake in the oven for 13–15 minutes, until risen and golden. A skewer inserted into the centre of a muffin should come out clean.

Remove from the oven and leave to cool for 10 minutes, then transfer to a wire cooling rack and leave to cool completely before covering with icing.

Once they are cool, ice the cupcakes with any of the icing recipes overleaf.

CUPCAKE ICINGS

Cupcake icing can be overly-sweet and sickly so I much prefer this lighter recipe, as I don't suffer from a shaky, sugary high afterwards. If you love dairy, use full-fat cream cheese, but I often use the dairy-free version as it works just as well. Simply add different flavours to your base to give your cupcakes more personality. The coconut cream icing from my cherry berry sponge cake (page 178) also works a treat.

BASIC ICING

250g dairy-free or regular cream cheese

4 tbsp set honey

100g coconut oil, melted

Put the cream cheese and honey into a food processor and blitz until smooth. With the motor running, pour in the melted coconut oil and blitz briefly until fully incorporated.

When you are ready to serve, ice the cupcakes using a spoon or piping bag, then arrange on a serving plate.

FOR LAVENDER & HONEY ICING

Buds from 3 fresh unsprayed lavender stems, or 2½ tsp dried lavender (available in the spice section of good supermarkets)

Runny honey, for drizzling

Follow the steps to make the Basic Icing and, once ready, remove the icing from the processor and stir in most of the lavender buds until combined. Cover and refrigerate for 2–3 hours until completely set.

When you are ready to serve, ice the cupcakes using a spoon or piping bag then arrange on a serving plate. To decorate, scatter over the remaining lavender. Serve immediately, or keep refrigerated until ready to serve.

FOR DRIED APPLE & CINNAMON ICING

½ tsp ground cinnamon, plus extra for dusting
Dried apple, to decorate

Add the cinnamon to the food processor and blitz for a few seconds to incorporate it with the icing. Transfer to a bowl, cover and refrigerate for 2–3 hours until completely set. When you are ready to serve, ice the cupcakes using a spoon or piping bag then arrange on a serving plate. To decorate, add a piece of dried apple to the top of each cupcake and dust with a little extra cinnamon. Serve immediately, or keep refrigerated until ready to serve.

FOR LEMON ICING

Finely grated zest of 3 unwaxed lemons
Candied lemon (optional)

Add the lemon zest to the food processor and blitz for a few seconds to incorporate it into the icing. Transfer to a bowl, cover and refrigerate for 2–3 hours until completely set.

When you are ready to serve, ice the cupcakes using a spoon or piping bag then arrange on a serving plate. To decorate, top with a few slices of candied lemon peel. Serve immediately, or keep refrigerated until ready to serve.

To say I have a sweet tooth is an understatement. I've been like this forever, and at one point it felt like my teeth were made of sugar cubes, and I dreamt of toffee-coated apples and chocolate dripping from spoons. When I was growing up, sugar was seen as the most wonderful treat and I think many of us '80s kids were rewarded with the sweet stuff if we ate all our dinner or did something remotely pleasing. This was the era of Global Hypercolour T-shirts, luminous fizzy drinks and the choc-ice.

Times have changed, and sugar is starting to be viewed in a different light. It has become less of a treat and more of a guaranteed way to put on weight, make you feel sluggish and alter your mood. After I had my son Rex I felt like a sloth and wanted to get my energy back. I quit refined sugar and after two weeks of slight withdrawal symptoms I felt incredible. With no more ups and downs in energy, the baby weight gradually and naturally came off and I had more of a twinkle in my eye.

Luckily for me and my sweet-toothed compatriots out there, there are many delicious refined sugar alternatives such as dates, coconut sugar, maple syrup and xylitol, that mean you can still have treats, but ones that will work with your body instead of against it.

You may not be acquainted with all of these refined sugar alternatives, so this chapter keeps it simple and offers readily available substitutes that taste divine. You won't need to compromise on flavour but you will notice how differently your body reacts to the food. You'll feel light and full of energy.

Making sweet treats feels like true alchemy for an untrained yet passionate cook like myself. The recipes in this chapter aren't over-complicated but they look picture-perfect and taste unreal. I urge you not to disclose the ingredients to your dinner guests or friends until after they've devoured them all. Most won't believe the lack of naughty stuff and how good they taste.

These goodies are also a handy way of getting more nutrients into your diet, with plenty of fruit crammed in for good measure. And they're a sure-fire method of getting your kids to eat fruit, too. So sweet stuff can be GOOD.

Now, instead of toffee apples, I dream of coconut truffles and refined sugar-free mango 'cheesecake'!

Desserts
&
Treats

MINI COCONUT & CHERRY TARTS

MAKES 6 MINI TARTS

These would be my desert island dessert essential. They look divine, taste so naughty but are pure goodness, and they're fun to make too. They make the perfect tea party centrepiece, and your friends won't believe they are good for you!

For the base:
100g raw unsalted almonds
90g plain oatcakes
90g dried dates, pitted
1 tbsp coconut oil
4 tsp unsweetened cocoa powder
2 tsp maple syrup
Pinch of sea salt

For the filling:
2 x 400ml cans full-fat coconut milk, chilled
3 tbsp set honey
½ tsp vanilla extract
Pinch of sea salt
18 fresh cherries, halved and pitted
50g raw unsalted pistachio nuts, cut into slivers

Preheat the oven to 200°C/180°C fan/400°F/Gas mark 6 and line the holes of a 6-hole muffin tray with cling film.

To make the base, place the almonds in a roasting tray and roast for 5–6 minutes, or until a shade darker and aromatic, taking care not to let them burn. Remove from the oven and leave to cool. Place all the ingredients for the base, including the roasted almonds, in the bowl of a food processor and blitz until the mixture forms a paste that sticks together when you press it between your fingers.

Divide the base mixture between the 6 lined muffin holes, pressing it firmly into the base and sides. Place in the freezer for 20 minutes, to set firm. Once firm, remove the tray and carefully lift up the overhanging cling film from each hole to release the mini tart cases. Place the tart cases on a plate, cover and chill.

Remove the cans of coconut milk from the fridge without shaking. Remove the lids and carefully scoop out the very firm, set coconut cream at the top, leaving the coconut water in the cans (don't throw the water away – use it to make soups, curries, porridge or smoothies). Add the thick coconut cream to the cleaned-out bowl of the food processor together with the honey, vanilla extract and salt and blitz until completely smooth. Remove the tart cases from the fridge and evenly divide the coconut cream between them. Add three cherry halves to the top of each mini tart and scatter over the slivered pistachio nuts. Serve immediately or chill, covered, for up to 3 days (or until ready to serve).

FROZEN BANANA & RASPBERRY ICE CREAM

SERVES 2

This is the easiest ice cream in the world to make and it's so delicious, you'll never want the shop-bought variety again. I love making this for the kids as I know exactly what's in it and there are no nasties – just fruity goodness and protein from the almonds.

3 ripe bananas

150g frozen raspberries, or buy fresh and freeze them yourself

2 tbsp almond milk (page 50 or shop-bought)

1 tbsp almond butter (page 30 or shop-bought)

Toppings:

Granola (page 34 or shop-bought)

Chia, sunflower or pumpkin seeds

Goji berries

Toasted flaked almonds

A few fresh raspberries

The day before you want to make the ice cream, peel the bananas, cut them into bite-sized chunks, place the chunks in a freezer bag and freeze. If you have fresh raspberries, pop them in the freezer too.

When you are ready to make the ice cream, remove the bananas and raspberries from the freezer and leave to thaw for 5 minutes. Place them in the bowl of a food processor or a blender and blitz for 1 minute, until they are finely ground. Add the almond milk and nut butter and blitz for a further minute, or until it is smooth and creamy.

Transfer to bowls and serve immediately with whatever toppings you like.

KIDS' BLUEBERRY & MANGO ICE LOLLIES

MAKES 6 ICE LOLLIES

Rex is never far from the freezer, as he knows these will always be there waiting for him. Luckily they're packed with goodness, so you know that as well as enjoying a sweet treat your kids are getting a tonne of fruit in them at the same time (they contain no nasties, unlike so many shop-bought lollies). I love eating them in the summertime too, as they're so refreshing, and easy and cheap to make.

2 ripe bananas, peeled
100g blueberries
150g ripe mango flesh
400ml coconut water

Put all of the ingredients in the bowl of a food processor or a high-speed blender and blitz until completely smooth. Divide the mixture between 6 ice-lolly moulds and freeze until almost solid. Insert ice-lolly sticks and return to the freezer until completely solid. Store in the freezer until ready to serve.

TROPICAL PINEAPPLE ICE LOLLIES

MAKES 6 ICE LOLLIES

If you find it a challenge to get enough fruit into your children's diets, these lollies are perfect. Rex would chose an ice lolly over pretty much any food, so I've had fun playing with flavours and ingredients as a way to get those vitamins into him. Fear not though, this is a dreamy lolly for any age. I found them soothing when I was pregnant during a particularly hot summer. One taste and you're transported to a hot tropical beach.

300g frozen pineapple chunks
300ml coconut milk
1 tbsp honey or maple syrup (optional)
½ a ripe banana, peeled
Grated zest of 1 lime
1 tsp vanilla extract

Put all of the ingredients into the bowl of a food processor or a high-speed blender and blitz until completely smooth. Divide the mixture between 6 ice-lolly moulds and freeze until almost solid. Insert ice-lolly sticks and return to the freezer until completely solid. Store in the freezer until ready to serve.

CHOCOLATE SHARDS

SERVES 6

Making your own chocolate may sound daunting, but in fact it's beyond easy and so delicious. I much prefer this to the shop-bought stuff as not only is it free from dairy and refined sugar, you can tailor it to your own taste. The shards keep well in the fridge so are perfect for a quick sweet fix and gorgeous for decorating the top of a cake, making it look like a work of art (see my death by chocolate cake, page 185). If you can't find cacao butter, use extra coconut oil, but remember it is softer and melts more easily, so the shards must be kept in the freezer or fridge, then removed 5 minutes before serving. The cacao butter gives them more of a 'snap' like real chocolate, but they should still be kept in the fridge and taken out just before serving.

60g cacao butter

40g coconut oil

50g raw cacao powder or unsweetened cocoa powder

60ml maple syrup

Good pinch of flaked sea salt

Optional toppings:
Dried cranberries
Goji berries
Desiccated coconut
Toasted flaked almonds
Pistachio nuts

Line a 22 x 18cm baking tray with baking parchment. If you use a smaller baking tray, the shards will be thicker.

Melt the cacao butter and coconut oil in a heat-proof bowl placed over a pan of simmering water, making sure the base of the bowl does not touch the water. Once melted, remove from the heat and whisk in the cacao or cocoa powder and maple syrup until smooth.

Pour the mixture on to the lined baking tray and smooth it out. Sprinkle over the sea salt and whatever toppings you like, cover with cling film and transfer to the freezer to set for at least 30 minutes.

When you are ready to serve the shards, remove the tray from the freezer and leave the chocolate to thaw for 10 minutes (this makes it easier to cut the chocolate into clean 'shards'). Cut and serve immediately, as it quickly softens. Store any uneaten shards (not very likely!) in the fridge (for up to 2 weeks) or freezer (for a couple of months).

RAW COCONUT TRUFFLES

MAKES 22 BALLS

I could eat a whole batch of these in one go. They are a moreish, sin-free sweet treat. You may have seen similar truffles in shops and cafés but they'll likely be overpriced and will never taste as good as the ones you can make at home. Easy and quick to prepare, these truffles make a great snack for when you're on the go or at work. They can be kept in the fridge in an airtight container for up to 2 weeks, for when you're having an energy slide.

50g raw unsalted cashew nuts

150g desiccated coconut, plus extra to coat

2 tbsp coconut oil

8 Medjool dates, pitted

¼ tsp ground cinnamon

Pinch of sea salt

Place all the ingredients in the bowl of a food processor and blitz for about 1 minute, or until the mixture sticks together when you press it between your fingers.

Shape the mixture into 22 balls and roll each ball in desiccated coconut to coat. Store in an airtight container in the fridge.

CHOCOLATE TOFFEE TRUFFLES

MAKES 12–14 BALLS

Chocolate . . . my hero food. I have been in love with the stuff since I was a kid and, like my addiction to new shoes, I have inherited this from my mother. These truffles are creamy, luxurious and decadent. The apricots give them a wonderful toffee flavour and perfectly complement the chocolate. You can fool most kids with these as you'd never know they were free from refined-sugar. They keep well in an airtight container in the fridge for up to 1 week.

12 unsulphured dried apricots

40g raw unsalted almonds

1½ tbsp almond butter (page 30 or shop-bought)

2 tbsp coconut oil

For the chocolate coating:

80g dark chocolate (minimum 70 per cent cocoa solids)

Or:

5 tbsp coconut oil, melted

3 tbsp raw cacao powder or unsweetened cocoa powder

1 tbsp maple syrup

½ tsp vanilla extract

Sunflower oil, for greasing

Edible glitter, for sprinkling (optional)

Grease a plate with a few drops of sunflower oil and set aside.

Put the dried apricots, almonds, almond butter and coconut oil in the bowl of a food processor and blitz until the mixture forms a paste that sticks together when you press it between your fingers. Shape the mixture into 12–14 balls (roughly one heaped teaspoon for each ball). Transfer the balls to the greased plate, cover with clingfilm and place in the freezer for 15 minutes.

Meanwhile, melt the dark chocolate in a heatproof bowl set over barely simmering water, or combine all the coating ingredients in a bowl, mixing thoroughly until smooth. Remove the balls from the freezer and, using a toothpick, dip the balls, one at a time, into the chocolate coating, until they're completely covered. Carefully place them back on the greased plate and return to the freezer for a further 10 minutes until set.

Remove the balls from the freezer, give them a second coating of chocolate (if using), and return to the plate. Chill for 1 hour to set. Serve piled in little bowls, and dust with edible glitter if you like.

MANGO CHEESECAKE

SERVES 12

We're serious mango-holics in our house so this cake goes down a storm. The pretty layers packed with creaminess make this a luxurious pud to tickle the taste buds. It covers many nutritional bases too, as you're getting vitamin C from the mango, good fats and protein from the nuts and lashings of fibre from the dates. Serve it up after dinner or keep it in the freezer for an ice-cold snack whenever the moment strikes. If you use maple syrup rather than honey, it becomes vegan.

For the base:
150g raw unsalted almonds
100g dried dates, pitted
1 tbsp coconut oil
Pinch of sea salt

For the filling:
400g raw unsalted cashew nuts, soaked in plenty of water for 6 hours or overnight
½ tsp fine sea salt
Grated zest of 1 unwaxed lemon, plus 3½ tbsp juice
180g honey or maple syrup
140g coconut oil, melted
1 tsp vanilla extract

For the mango layer:
Flesh of 1 large, ripe mango (about 200g), plus extra to serve (optional)
2 tbsp coconut oil, melted

To make the base, place all the ingredients in the bowl of a food processor and blitz until the mixture forms a paste that sticks together when you press it between your fingers. Press the mixture firmly into a 22cm round springform cake tin. Transfer to the freezer for 15 minutes to set.

To make the filling, drain the cashew nuts, place them in the bowl of a food processor or in a high-speed blender, and blitz to form a paste. Add the remaining filling ingredients and blitz until everything is well combined. Remove the set base from the freezer, pour the filling over it and smooth it out. Return the cake tin to the freezer for 10 minutes while you blitz the mango.

Rinse out the food processor bowl or blender, then add the mango flesh and blitz until smooth. Pour in the melted coconut oil and blitz again until combined. Pour the mango mixture over the cake, smooth the surface, cover and chill for at least 6 hours (ideally overnight).

Serve the cake in slices, with a little wedge of mango on top if you like.

It can be stored in an airtight container in the fridge for up to 2 days, or in the freezer for up to a month.

CHOCOLATE CRISPY CAKES

MAKES 20

These are never around for long in our house as they're Rex's favourite recipe from the book. They're perfect served at a children's party but also delicious with a cup of coffee mid-afternoon – Jesse can testify to this! The first time I experimented with these, when I took them out of the fridge, I saw that a thick layer of chocolate had settled at the base. I then realised this was an added bonus, making them a bit more decadent. The more sophisticated crispy cake, if you will.

200g coconut oil

150g raw cacao powder or unsweetened cocoa powder

100g maple syrup or honey

1 tsp vanilla extract

Good pinch of fine sea salt

150g sugar-free rice puffs

2 tbsp desiccated coconut, to decorate

Heat the coconut oil in a saucepan over a very low heat, stirring until just melted, then immediately remove from the heat. Whisk in the cacao powder, maple syrup or honey, vanilla extract and sea salt.

Combine the chocolate sauce and rice puffs in a bowl until thoroughly coated. Spoon the mixture into the paper cases, sprinkle with the desiccated coconut, and chill. They will keep in an airtight container in the fridge for up to 3 days.

FRUIT WHIP

SERVES 4

I created this dessert in a Mad Professor style. I had heard you could use silken tofu in puddings so got to work blending up different flavour combinations. Tofu is a perfect healthy base to replace the cream you would normally use in a dessert like this, and once set, it has a gorgeous, creamy, dreamy texture. It looks very alluring served up in a glass dish after dinner, but I sometimes eat it for breakfast as it's packed with fruit, and the tofu is a brilliant source of protein. You can make it up to a day in advance, so it's super-convenient, too.

400g silken tofu

100g blueberries, plus extra to serve

2 ripe nectarines or peaches, halved and stones removed

10 dried unsulphured apricots

2 tbsp coconut oil, melted

100ml almond milk (page 50 or shop-bought) or coconut milk

Grated zest of 1 unwaxed lemon

Pinch of sea salt

Put all of the ingredients (except one of the nectarines) in the bowl of a food processor or in a high-speed blender and blitz until completely smooth. Divide the mixture between 4 small glasses, cover and chill for at least 2 hours.

When ready to serve, cut the remaining nectarine into little wedges. Top each glass with blueberries and wedges of nectarine and serve.

LEMON CASHEW BALLS

MAKES 18-20 BALLS

I love the zingy taste of lemon, and these are mouth-wateringly fresh. If you're not a confident baker, give them a go – they are raw and so easy to make. I always have a batch of them in the fridge so I can grab a couple when I need a sweet pick-me-up. You'll only find natural sugars in these balls, which give you a steady release of energy. They can be kept in an airtight container in the fridge for up to 2 weeks and in the freezer for up to 2 months.

100g raw unsalted cashew nuts
6 Medjool or 10 regular dates, pitted
Grated zest of 1 unwaxed lemon
2 tbsp desiccated coconut
1 tbsp coconut oil, melted
1 tbsp chia seeds
Small pinch of sea salt

Place all the ingredients in the bowl of a food processor and blitz for 1 minute, or until the mixture sticks together when you press it between your fingers.

Shape the mixture into 18–20 balls (roughly 1 heaped teaspoon for each). Store in an airtight container in the fridge or freezer.

INDEX

Big thanks to all the lovely people who contributed
tirelessly to the styling and props at the photoshoots:

Hair: Lisa Eastwood
Make-up: Justine Jenkins
Styling: Sinead McKeefry

Smeg, Anthropologie, Talking Tables, Sophie Allport,
Lights4fun, Oliver Bonas, Lavinia's Tea Party, Forest
& Co, Fired Earth, Melody Rose, Elan Bach, Barnaby
Gates, RE, Stylish Life, Jimbob Art, Mrs Moore,
Cali Rand and Liberty, with special thanks to
Charlotte Knott

THANK YOU!

I finish this book from a place of pure gratitude as I'm filled with love that this dream has become a reality. Thank you Orion for making this happen: Amanda Harris and Tamsin English, you are a joy to work with and I'm over the moon that you embraced my ideas and brought them to life.

Cheers to the Irish dream that is Jordan Bourke who not only helped me fine-tune my recipes but taught me so much along the way. Cooking with you in my kitchen was a total privilege.

Thanks to Rowan Lawton from Furniss Lawton at the James Grant Group for loving food as much as me and for pushing me in the right direction and getting those early dreams focused.

Thank you to my dear mate Jesse May Underwood for the delicious illustrations. It's been so wonderful to get to work with an old friend and to keep this book in the family.

Thank you to Tamin Jones for bringing the whole book to life with exceptional photography. The food jumps off the page due to your incredible understanding of how to shoot it. Thanks Rebecca Newport for gathering the most exquisite array of crockery, utensils and other props for our shoot. I'm so glad you have the same enthusiasm as I do for all things colourful and kitsch.

A massive thanks to my husband, children, stepkids, mum, dad, brother and all the visitors to our gaff for giving me great, honest feedback on my recipes and for always being willing guinea pigs.

Lastly a gargantuan thanks to YOU for buying the book and for cooking happy and healthy.

First published in Great Britain in 2016
by Orion Publishing Group Ltd

Carmelite House, 50 Victoria Embankment
London EC4Y 0DZ

An Hachette UK Company

10 9 8 7 6 5 4 3 2

A CIP catalogue record for this book
is available from the British Library.

ISBN: 978-1-409-16375-6

Photography: Tamin Jones
Design: Anita Mangan
Illustrations: Jessica May Underwood

Props: Rebecca Newport
Recipe development and food styling: Jordan Bourke
Garden design: Cali Rand

Printed and bound in Germany

*Note: While every effort has been made to ensure
that the information in this book is correct, it should
not be substituted for medical advice. It is the sole
responsibility of the reader to determine which foods
are safe to consume. If you are concerned about any
aspect of your health, speak to your GP.*

The Orion Publishing Group's policy is to use
papers that are natural, renewable and recyclable
products and made from wood grown in sustainable
forests. The logging and manufacturing processes
are expected to conform to the environmental
regulations of the country of origin.

www.orionbooks.co.uk

by
BOOK
or by
COOK
COOKING
EATING
SHARING

For more delicious recipes,
features, videos and exclusives
from Orion's cookery writers,
and to sign up for our 'Recipe
of the Week' email visit
bybookorbycook.co.uk